# TO MAKE A POET BLACK

# To Make a Poet Black

*J. SAUNDERS REDDING*

WITH AN INTRODUCTION BY

HENRY LOUIS GATES, JR.

*Cornell University Press*

ITHACA AND LONDON

*Library of Congress Cataloging-in-Publication Data*
Redding. J. Saunders (Jay Saunders), 1906–1988
  To make a poet Black.

  Includes index.
    1. American poetry—Afro-American authors—History
and criticism.  2. American literature—Afro-American
authors—History and criticism.  3. Afro-Americans–
Intellectual life.  I. Title.
PS153.N5R4  1987    811'.009'896073    86-47630
ISBN 0-8014-1982-4
ISBN 0-8014-9438-9 (pbk.)

Introduction copyright © 1988 by Henry Louis Gates, Jr.

First published 1939 by the University of North Carolina Press.
Cornell University Press cloth and paper editions first published 1988.

Printed in the United States of America

*The paper in this book is acid-free and meets the guidelines for
permanence and durability of the Committee on Production Guidelines
for Book Longevity of the Council on Library Resources.*

To
my Father
and
the memory of
my Mother

# "... and bid him sing": J. Saunders Redding and the Criticism of American Negro Literature

BY HENRY LOUIS GATES, JR.

> Yet do I marvel at this curious thing:
> To make a poet black, and bid him sing!
> —Countee Cullen

J. Saunders Redding (1906–1988), the author of eight books and more than three dozen essays, and the editor of an anthology of Afro-American literature that remains widely used, was the veritable dean of Afro-American literary critics. Indeed, for many black professors of English and American Studies, Redding was the model of the Afro-American scholar-critic. The often-noted elegance of his mind, his morals, and his critical works made him the walking embodiment of the black tradition's aspirations toward academic excellence.

Among the honors and achievements that graced Redding's eight-odd decades, two stand high in the list: his occupancy of Cornell University's Ernest I. White Professorship of American Studies and Humane Letters, which made Redding the first Afro-American to hold an endowed professorship in literary criticism at an Ivy League university; and the publication in 1939 of *To Make a Poet Black*, which Redding's biographer, Pancho Savery, calls "the first comprehensive [and] serious critical work devoted exclusively to Afro-American literature and written by an Afro-American." It is in anticipation of the fiftieth anniversary of the publication of *To Make a Poet Black* that Cornell University Press is reissuing this canonical work of Afro-American literary criticism. Most regrettably, Saunders Redding died while the work was in press, and thus a project conceived as a tribute to him must instead serve as a tribute to his memory.

Redding was born in Wilmington, Delaware, in 1906, the third of seven children in what he properly calls "an upper-class Negro family." Both his parents were graduates of Howard University. His father, Lewis Alfred, served as the secretary of the Wilmington branch of the NAACP and founded the first black YMCA in Wilmington. His mother, Mary Ann Holmes, as Redding tells us in his autobiography, *No Day of Triumph* (1942), taught him and his siblings the lost art of oratory and introduced them, through oral readings, to the canonical works of the Western tradition and also to the poetry of Paul Laurence Dunbar. Dunbar's widow, Alice Dunbar-Nelson, a pioneering figure in Afro-American women's literature, was Redding's English teacher at Wilmington's all-black Howard High School.

Upon graduation at the age of sixteen, Redding attended Lincoln University in Pennsylvania for one year before matriculating at Brown University, from which his older brother, Louis, who went on to become a lawyer, had graduated. There Saunders Redding earned the Ph.B. degree in English in 1928 and an M.A. in English in 1932. In 1929, he married Esther Elizabeth James, a teacher (they had two sons, Conway and Lewis). He taught at Morehouse College in Atlanta between 1928 and 1931, at Louisville Municipal College in 1934–1936, and at Southern University at New Orleans in 1936–1938, then moving to Eliz-

abeth City (North Carolina) State Teachers College until
1943. In that year he joined the faculty at Hampton Institute, where he was named the Johnson Professor of Creative Literature in 1955 and remained until 1967. In 1949–
1950, he served as visiting professor at Brown, becoming
the first black person ever to teach at an Ivy League university. He was later a fellow in humanities at Duke, in 1964–
1965. Between 1966 and 1970, Redding served as director
of the Division of Research and Publication of the National
Endowment for the Humanities. During his last two years
in that post he was also professor of American History and
Civilization at George Washington University. In 1970, he
moved to Cornell, where he retired as Ernest I. White
Professor Emeritus. Among his many honors were mem-
bership in Phi Beta Kappa, a Rockefeller Foundation fel-
lowship, the Mayflower Award, and two Guggenheim fellowships. He also lectured in India (1952) under the
auspices of the State Department, and served as an American Society for African Culture exchange lecturer in Africa, where he met and became an intimate friend of Wole
Soyinka, the 1986 Nobel Laureate in Literature.

Although these bare facts suggest something of the
range and depth of Redding's career, they do nothing to
suggest the complexity of a man whose ideal was to embody the black tradition's ultimate title, "a race man," a
man who was fired from his position at the prestigious
black college, Morehouse, because a conservative admin-
istration found him "too radical," a man who could write
that, at Brown, "I hated and feared the whites" and simultaneously "hated and feared and was ashamed of
Negroes," a man who was a pioneering crusader for the
civil rights of Afro-Americans yet of whom Amiri Baraka
(LeRoi Jones) could allow himself to write in 1984 that his
public opinions were "basically supportive of the oppres-

sion of the Afro-American nation and white chauvinism in general."

We can come to a fuller understanding of Redding's complex views about race by recalling that he embodied the black tradition's emphasis upon rugged individual attainment in overcoming what to our generation of black scholars seem like insuperable barriers imposed by vulgar and comprehensive racism, as if "the race," as we once called our ethnicity, could progress only through the individual successes of unimpeachable exemplars, of which Redding was one. Simultaneously, we must recall that Redding—and the entire generation of black scholars to which he belonged—saw the urge to segregate anything black, as well as the urge among black nationalists to codify and celebrate our cultural difference, as politically conservative, at best, and as politically retrograde and irresponsible, at worst. We can see these two tensions come to bear on Redding's thought throughout his work. As he told an audience at Brown in June 1968, during his Phi Beta Kappa address, "Preferential treatment must be accorded the Negro and other disadvantaged minorities if 'racial equality' is not to remain a delusion. . . . [However, the] Negro American . . . is no more African than the fairest Anglo-Saxon Protestant is. . . . His destiny is one with the destiny of America. . . . Let us not deceive ourselves. As the comic strip character, Pogo, once remarked, 'We have seen the enemy, and they is us.' " Such statements embody the classic black civil rights ideology widely current from the creation of the Niagara Movement in 1905 until the Black Power/Black Arts movement came into being in the mid-sixties. It was for holding that position that Redding was fired from Morehouse in 1931 and subsequently attacked by conservatives both white and black. For continuing to hold it, though honored in 1945 by the Urban

League "for outstanding achievement" as an advocate of
civil rights, he was attacked in the late sixties by blacks who
properly celebrated the African heritage implicit in the
term "Afro-American," and who saw the creation of Black
Studies departments as the logical outgrowth of the civil
rights movement, and indeed of the academic and political
careers of exemplary "race men and women"—of which no
more outstanding example existed than J. Saunders Redding. The curious reversal of the perception of Redding's
political beliefs over the past half century—from "radical"
to "conservative"—reflects the irony and paradox of Afro-
American intellectual thought in the twentieth century.

Some of Redding's own autobiographical passages help
the contemporary reader to understand the origins and
development of the history of his ideology about race. "My
parents," Redding wrote in his entry in *Twentieth Century
Authors* (First Supplement, 1955),

> were far from being either rich or poor. Both were reli-
> gious, of profound Christian faith, but "faith without
> works" is no good. So they worked—my mother at home,
> my father at many things, but principally at his job in the
> postal service, which was the steady source of our income.
> My parents taught their children to work too. I remember
> the first three of us in the evening after dinner, washing
> and drying the dishes while our mother sat on the step that
> led down from the dining room and read aloud to us. She
> loved to read and we loved to listen to Hans Christian
> Andersen, Paul Dunbar, Longfellow, Shakespeare, 'The
> Tragic Story of the Titanic,' and selections from the *World's
> Famous Orations*, including Greek and Roman orations. We
> were taught the declining art of elocution.

Redding's own understanding of the way the heinous
particularity of white racism worked upon his parents, and
ultimately upon himself and his siblings, bears repeating:

As far back as I can remember, it was necessary for my father to eke out his small government salary by doing all sorts of odd jobs after his regular hours and during his vacations. . . . As I look back upon it now, I know that my father was driven by more than the necessity to provide a living for his family. Surrounded by whites both at home and at work, he was driven by an intangible something, a merciless, argus-eyed spiritual enemy that stalked his every movement and lurked in every corner. It goaded him every waking hour, but he could not get at it, though he felt it to be embodied in almost every white man he met. Because of this he moved with defensive caution, calculating the effect of every action and every utterance upon his unseen enemy. Every day he won defensive victories, but every day the final victory seemed more impossible. He was up at dawn, painting the trim, repairing the roof, putting out the ashes, shoveling snow from the sidewalk. In fifteen years he was never late for work, and only once did he allow an illness to keep him home. His endurance was a thing of spirit.

But it was as a student at Brown that Redding's ideas about race and writing were shaped most fully. As the author of Redding's entry in *Current Biography* (1969) put it,

In *No Day of Triumph*, Redding recalled how his feelings of alienation were exacerbated at Brown. The handful of Negro students on campus avoided each other in public, and when they met clandestinely it was not to discuss the snubs they received and other racial problems but rather to seek escape in parties with Negro students from nearby colleges. In his senior year, when he was the only black student at Brown, he began to feel that he was "fighting the whole white world" singlehandedly. "I hated and feared the whites," he wrote. "I hated and feared and was ashamed of Negroes." But it was at Brown that he sought refuge and outlet for these emotions about racism in writing. "It was at college that I began to give serious attention to writing, not as a career but because I liked it; though only heaven knows why, since even then the effort used to tear me apart," he recounted in his contribution to *Twentieth Century Authors.* "But I wrote reams and reams, and got taken on by the *Brown Literary Quarterly,* and worshiped Sid (S. J.) Perelman, who was on the *Brown Jug,* and read everything, and finally, in my senior year, got a letter from H. L. Mencken telling me to try again, and another letter from Eugene Jolas, way over in Paris, telling me that *Transition* was going to publish my story 'Delaware Coon.'"

But because his father thought that "Delaware Coon" was an embarrassment to the entire race, Redding stopped trying to publish until a ten-year silence was broken splendidly in 1939 by the publication of *To Make a Poet Black.*

Contemplating the awesome task of writing a formal history of the African-American tradition of imaginative literature, Jay Saunders Redding did not wince. Nor did he succumb to the easy temptation of the chronological catalog, the listing of authors' names, dates, titles of works, and the sort of useful summary of plot and theme designed to introduce the novice and the nonspecialist to the fullest range of black authors and their works within the broadest of frames. Works such as these were inclusive and documentary, rather than inclusive and critical. The great service that they performed was to preserve the names of authors and their work. Rather than supplement or refine the three or four broad, inclusive works of "listings" which he inherited, however, Redding sought to do something else. Going well beyond the model of the inclusive testimony to the existence of our authors, their lives, and works—aimed most polemically at those who would deny our voiced presence as citizens in the republic of letters—Redding introduced a bold and imaginative new form into the Afro-American critical tradition. And that innovative form we might profitably think of as an *exclusive* literary history, our tradition's very first sophisticated exercise in canon formation. Redding, in writing *To Make a Poet Black*, sought to chart the contours of the canon of the black tradition.

In one very important sense, Redding seems to have had rather little choice. Great works of lovingly detailed and diligent literary archaeology had preceded him, leaving him very little room in which to maneuver to create an *original* statement about black literature. Because Redding's *To Make a Poet Black* can be read as a revision or rewriting of works the genre of which is best represented by Benjamin Brawley's work, it is important to understand what Brawley did. Brawley's *The Negro in Literature and Art in the United States,* published in 1918 and in four revised editions by 1930, boldly and squarely broke the critical silence about the black aesthetic tradition by asserting its existence. Brawley argued passionately, if not too persuasively, about an entity he called "the Negro Genius," then traced its manifestations in the written works of Phillis Wheatley, Paul Laurence Dunbar, W. E. B. Du Bois, William Stanley Braithwaite, James Weldon Johnson (each of whom receives a full chapter of analysis), the spoken words of Frederick Douglass and Booker T. Washington, the painting of Henry O. Tanner, and the sculpture of Meta Warrick Fuller. Brawley supplements these careful readings with broader chapters on "Other Writers" before the Harlem Renaissance and "the New Realists" of the Renaissance itself. A sweeping and lyrical chapter entitled "Music," ranges in concern from the classical works of Samuel Coleridge-Taylor and George Bridgetower of the late and early nineteenth century, respectively, to the popular "cross-over" compositions of Harry T. Burleigh and the internationally popular tenor Roland Hayes.

Brawley's artistic sweep was wide, his political intentions precise, and he stated his thesis plainly. His ideological concern was to demonstrate that black people in America have "peculiar gifts which need all possible cultivation and which will some day add to the glory of the country" (p. 8), and these "gifts" manifest themselves "primarily in the field of aesthetics" (p. 4). Negro Americans had much to give to a still nascent American civilization, if America would only cultivate these largely dormant gifts, gifts that still existed primarily in the realm of possibility because of the Negro's "economic instability." If the status of the Negro American is enhanced, if the limits upon individual and group possibility are lifted, then Brawley maintains, optimistically, "the possibilities of the race in literature and music, in painting and sculpture, are illimitable" (p. 9).

If these were Brawley's ideological intentions in writing *The Negro in Literature and Art,* his intellectual intention was equally clear, and far more fertile. Brawley concludes his work by revealing his wish for the impact that his pioneering testament to "the Negro Genius" might have upon subsequent black authors, indeed upon the black tradition in letters itself. "Let us hope," he writes, "that those who come after may be worthy of the great tradition" (p. 182). There it is, that haunting phrase which F. R. Leavis in 1948 would assert to define *his* canon of the best in the English novel. Brawley sought nothing less than to *assert* the existence of this "great" black aesthetic tradition and, by thus giving it formal, critical birth, begin its codification. Few gestures in the history of black criticism are as grand or as salient as was Brawley's.

*To Make a Poet Black* builds on Brawley's work as well as on the critical works of Vernon Loggins (*The Negro Author and His Development,* 1930) and Sterling A. Brown (*The Negro in American Literature,* 1935). But Redding took the tradition in a new direction. Although he has since written several works published to wide acclaim, none of his other books has been more important to the development of Afro-American literature as a valid subject of inquiry within traditional departments of English than has *To Make a Poet Black*. Indeed, it is fair to say, fifty years after its publication, that *To Make a Poet Black* is the first sophisticated book of literary criticism published about Afro-American literature, and that its author is the tradition's first eminent scholar-critic.

Why are we free to make such claims? Precisely because in this book Redding accomplished two major and original feats. First, he recognized that though a literary tradition consists of all the texts and authors that satisfy the criteria according to which that "tradition" might be broadly defined, it was the canonical authors of the black tradition, those whose works in some way most fully represented its salient aspects, who had to be identified. A canon, for Redding, was the marrow of tradition. Whereas virtually all his predecessors had deemed it essential to include in their surveys anyone of African-American descent who had published a literary work, Redding chose to concentrate on only the black tradition's *signal* works. He believed that his task, the task of the critic, was to draw distinctions, to make aesthetic judgments, to chart formal lines of descent. He includes in the canon the following authors: Jupiter Hammon, Phillis Wheatley, George Moses Horton, Charles Remond, William Wells Brown, Frederick Douglass, Frances Ellen Watkins, James Madison Bell, James E. Campbell, Paul Laurence Dunbar, Charles W. Chesnutt, W. Burghardt Du Bois, Fenton Johnson, William Stanley Braithwaite, Claude McKay, Jean Toomer, Jessie Fauset, Langston Hughes, Countee Cullen, Rudolph Fisher, and James Weldon Johnson, ending his study by pointing, prophetically, to "the gratifying new work of Sterling Brown in poetry and Zora Neale Hurston in prose." Redding's judgment is in all points measured, considered, sound.

Second, Redding, unlike Benjamin Brawley though in direct response to him, regards any attempt to base one's notion of tradition upon "racial temperament," a black "collective unconscious," or "Negro genius" as essentialist and ahistorical. Rather, he is concerned to demonstrate the links of formal influence and vision which connect the great works of a tradition like links in a chain. Frances Ellen Watkins's poetry, for instance, Redding argues, prefigures James Weldon Johnson's use of "dialectical patterns" (p. 43), while her profound opposition to "racial limitations of matter and method" heavily informed both Johnson's and Paul Laurence Dunbar's understanding of the nature and function of Afro-American literature. Redding, moreover, is concerned to show how black texts influence and are echoed by other black texts, because black authors read and respond to—in a sense, revise—other black authors. Unlike Sterling Brown, then, who in his critical work sought to record the elaborate interplay between *American* texts, white and black, Redding viewed the canon of the Afro-American tradition as, as it were, self-contained. J. Saunders Redding, in this book, defines a literary tradition based upon formal principles of what in the sixties came to be thought of as "cultural nationalism." Ironically, the black cultural nationalists considered Redding a racial conservative. Yet, it was Redding who first provided a *system* of criticism which formalized with impressive subtlety and irrefutable acumen the basis upon which any meaningful definition of a "black" tradition would have to be constructed.

Although this is not the place to examine all Redding's critical judgments, it will reward us to consider the salient aspects of his arguments about the nature and function of the black tradition. Black literature, he claims early on, "has been literature either of *purpose* or *necessity,* and it is because of this that it appeals as much to the cognitive as to the conative and affective side of man's being" (p. xxix, emphasis added). Black literature, in other words, is *committed,* a priori: "literary expression for the Negro has not been, and is not wholly now an art in the sense that the poetry and prose of another people, say the Irish, is art." Rather, black literature embodies at once the act of striving after an effect (or producing an *affect*), and the processes of "knowing" in the widest possible sense, including those of perception, memory, judgment, and the like. Long before the great African theorists of Negritude defined all black art as "functional" and "affective," Redding identified these two features as central to any definition of the Afro-American literary tradition.

Black literature, then, is a "literature of necessity," a literature produced to perform a political function as much as (if not more than) to embody an aesthetic one (p. 3). This political function has been to critique white racism and, simultaneously, to demonstrate the intellectual capacities of all black people through the agency of the artistic products of one black person, in a relation of a part standing for the whole.

All Afro-American literature is contained within twin necessities, which Redding defines as "the necessity of ends" and "the necessity of means." It is worthwhile to note the distinction that he draws between the two:

> Negro writers have been obliged to have two faces. If they wished to succeed they have been obliged to satisfy two different (and opposed when not entirely opposite) audiences, the black and the white. This necessity of means, perhaps, has been even stronger than the necessity of ends,

and as writers have increased, the necessity has grown almost to the point of desperation.

From Jupiter Hammon, the first Negro writer in America, to Countee Cullen and Langston Hughes, these two necessities can be traced with varying degrees of clarity— now one and now the other predominant—like threads through the whole cloth. With the very earliest writers the needs did not encompass more than personal self, but as consciousness of others awakened in later writers and as the simplicity of the Negro's primary position in America changed successively to the complexity of the times of abolition agitation, freedom, enfranchisement, and social self-determination the artless personality of his literature dropped away and he became the sometimes frenzied propagandist of racial consciousness and advancement. (Pp. 3–4]

It is difficult for contemporary readers to understand how novel, and bold, this distinction was. Precisely because of the double-sided code of necessity, most black intellectuals seemed to deem it improper to criticize black works of art in public discourse: such comments could be used by white racists in their continuing attempts to subjugate blacks. Redding not only criticizes this tendency, he also shows how and why it has come about. But, more important, he demonstrates, on formalistic grounds, which literature is worth emulating and which should be cast aside; which is peculiarly Afro-American, and which is not.

Redding's judgments are impressively sure. He seems equally concerned to stress aesthetic complexity and what we might think of as a form of ideological *integrity* in the ethnic experience of African-Americans. This, in fact, is a rather surprising aspect of Redding's criticism, given that contemporary readers encounter his work through the context of the black cultural nationalist critique of his supposed ideological "conservatism." Redding was indeed one of the very few early critics in the black tradition whose criticism expressed a "nationalist" ideology and aesthetic. Although this claim might be controversial, a simple reading of *To Make a Poet Black* can demonstrate what I mean by it. Redding's stress upon what I think of as the "self-contained" quality of literary influence among black authors is one instance of his "nationalism." As we shall see, the primacy that he grants the black oral tradition and the importance he gives to the growth of a free—and literate— black urban culture in the North are central components of his critical values.

For this reason he chastises Phillis Wheatley's work— certainly the most formally complex writing by a black author to appear until Jean Toomer published *Cane* (1923)—as "unracial," "unnatural," and "wan." It is, he argues, "this negative, bloodless, unracial quality . . . that makes her seem superficial, especially to members of her own race. . . . In this sense none of her poetry is real. Compared to the Negro writers who followed her, Miss Wheatley's passions are tame, her skill the sedulous copy of established techniques, and her thoughts the hand-me-downs of her age. She is chilly" (p. 11). Wheatley's poetry exemplifies no "dark bourne of flesh and blood" (p. 9). Aesthetic complexity without, as it were, *soul* or subject does not amount to a sufficiently *black* artistic artifact.

As would Sterling Brown in his monumental anthology *The Negro Caravan* (1941), Redding stresses the crucial role of the black vernacular in Afro-American literature. "The spirituals and prayers," he writes, "the sermons and work songs" are survivals of what he labels "this great body of folk literature." Indeed, Redding was the very first scholar to show that, in the first century of its existence, black literature in both North and South was essentially an oral literature. Privileging the oral, the vernacular, was a most unusual gesture for a black critic of Redding's generation. For many, the vernacular was a source of embarrassment: the linguistic and cultural remnant of African enslavement.

What Redding establishes in tracing the chain of influence from the anonymous oral literature of the nineteenth century to the poetry of Sterling Brown and the prose of Zora Hurston, by way of Frederick Douglass's oratory and the dialect poetry of Frances Ellen Watkins, Paul Laurence Dunbar, James Weldon Johnson, Langston Hughes, and Jean Toomer (with W. E. B. Du Bois—"a master of English prose and style" [p. 80]—and Charles Chesnutt amply acknowledged for their sophisticated prose), is a canon built upon a black vernacular foundation. This is Redding's "Great Tradition": a written tradition as an extension of the great, still unheralded black vernacular tradition. It is *this* claim, so subtly rendered, which is the most significant, and the boldest, insight of *To Make a Poet Black*, and which allows Redding's critical work to serve as the basis for the black post-structural theorizing of Houston A. Baker, Jr., and for black aesthetic theorizing such as that of Stephen Henderson.

Redding valorizes the oral throughout his text. Frederick Douglass, he points out, seems to write "for speech": "Douglass made no difference between the written and spoken word" (p. 33). Frances Ellen Watkins, he concludes, is memorable for her attempt to redirect the whole of the tradition away from propaganda and inward to an exploration of black spoken language. "In the volume called *Sketches of Southern Life*," he notes, "the language she puts in the mouths of Negro characters has a fine racy, colloquial tang" (p. 42). She was not writing in dialect, but she was making use of its speech patterns. Redding admired the "short, teethy, angry monosyllables" that she employed in her pieces on slavery (p. 43). His final judgment of her achievements is typical of his grace, balance, and judiciousness: "she gave to some of her pieces a lightness of touch that was sadly lacking in most of the heavy-footed writing of her race. A great deal of her poetry was written to be recited, and this led her into errors of metrical construction which, missed when the poems are spoken, show up painfully on the printed page. In all but her long, religious narrative, *Moses,* simplicity of thought and expression is the keystone" (p. 44).

Summarizing the tradition down to the turn of the century, Redding, though he chastises the writers both for a certain absence of artistry and for failing to understand the great potential of black vernacular forms for their art, praises those who helped to generate "a core of racial pride": "A great and good work was done. . . . Though they were not artists enough to see and recognize with love and pride the beauty of their own unaffected spirituals, tales, and work songs, they nevertheless acknowledged the possibilities for artistic treatment in Negro peasant life, the southern scene, and the enigmatic soul of the simple Negro" (p. 48).

Having shown how American minstrelsy and vaudeville had perverted for racist political ends the potential of the black vernacular as a medium for poetry, Redding goes on to demonstrate that both Dunbar and Chesnutt are important to the shaping of the tradition because they recuperated this potential. Dunbar, Redding writes, did not *imitate* the black vernacular; rather, he *produced* a poetic diction for the printed page; he "made a language, a synthetic dialect that could be read with ease and pleasure by the northern whites to whom dialect meant only an amusing burlesque of Yankee English. Through such a bastard medium," Redding concludes, "it was (and is) impossible to speak the whole heart of a people" (p. 63). Despite this crucial error, however, Dunbar "did his best work in this medium," and rescued "dialect poetry" from its racist denigrators. Chesnutt, "a transitional figure," at once consolidated the tradition in prose fiction between William Wells Brown and Dunbar and, like Dunbar, rescued dialect from the racist American stage. Similarly, Langston Hughes's importance related directly to his experiments with black language; these experiments saved the New Negro poets of the Harlem Renaissance from the "kinless verse" of the aracial poetry epitomized for Redding by the work of William Stanley Braithwaite, "the most outstanding example of perverted energy that the period from 1903 to 1917 produced" (p. 89), and by the claims and protestations of Countee Cullen about wishing to be a poet, and not a Negro poet of Negro verse. Of Cullen, Redding concludes, "when writing on race material Mr. Cullen is at his best. . . . And when he writes by it, he *writes;* but when this does not guide him, his pen trails faded ink across his pages." Cullen, at his worst, derives from Braithwaite at his best: "effete and bloodless" (pp. 108–9). Hughes, on the other hand, has turned to the vernacular, with promising, if not perfect, results: "he is a Negro divinely capable of realizing (which is instinctive) and giving expression to (which is cultivated) the dark perturbation of the soul—there is no other word—of the Negro. . . . More than any other writer of the race, Langston Hughes has been swept with this tide of feeling. This accounts for the fresh green of him, the variety of his moods." Nonetheless, though "he can catch up the dark messages of Negro feeling and express them in what he calls 'racial rhythms,' . . . it is as the iteration of the drum rather than the exposition of the piano. He feels in them, but he does not think. And this is the source of his naïvete" (pp. 115–16). Hughes's naïvete, however, is much less important than is his exemplification of a larger trend in the creation of a poetic diction that is vernacular-informed, vernacular-derived.

Redding ends *To Make a Poet Black* by arguing that the vernacular poetry and prose of James Weldon Johnson (in *God's Trombones*, 1927), Sterling Brown, and Zora Neale Hurston represent both the culmination of the tradition and the direction that the tradition must take to save itself from the folly of the pale imitation of forms and languages alien to it. He praises Johnson, for instance, whose work generates Brown's and Hurston's, for "discarding the mutilations of dialect," yet "retain[ing] the speech forms, the idea patterns, and the rich racial flavor" (p. 121). Finally, it is the turn "inward," the "return" to black language, and black forms, which will yield the most splendid results for the development of the tradition, just as similar turns and returns have done for other black artistic media, such as jazz and the blues: "It is this that must happen; a spiritual and physical return to the earth. For Negroes are yet an earthy people, a people earth-proud—the very salt of the earth. Their songs and stories have arisen from a loving bondage to the earth, and to it now they must return. It is to this, for pride, for strength, for endurance, that they must go back" (p. 124).

It is this central and original thread of reasoning, valorizing indigenously *black* forms, which confirms the legacy of *To Make a Poet Black*. For this novel thesis, elaborated upon in critical essays and creative works by Brown and Hurston, Stephen Henderson and Addison Gayle, Amiri Baraka and Larry Neal, Alice Walker and Toni Morrison, Houston Baker and myself, would become the very foundation for the quest to define a black aesthetic. The tradition's debt to the work of J. Saunders Redding will be difficult to repay.

# A J. Saunders Redding Bibliography

## BOOKS

*To Make a Poet Black.* Chapel Hill: University of North Carolina Press, 1939.

*No Day of Triumph.* New York: Harper, 1942.

*Stranger and Alone.* New York: Harcourt, Brace, 1950.

*They Came in Chains: Americans from Africa.* Philadelphia: Lippincott, 1950.

*On Being Negro in America.* Indianapolis: Bobbs-Merrill, 1951.

*An American in India: A Personal Report on the Indian Dilemma and the Nature of Her Conflicts.* Indianapolis: Bobbs-Merrill, 1954.

*The Lonesome Road: The Story of the Negro's Part in America.* Garden City, N.Y.: Doubleday, 1958.

*The Negro.* Washington, D.C.: Potomac Books, 1967.

## EDITED BOOKS

*Reading for Writing* (with Ivan E. Taylor). New York: Ronald Press, 1952.

*Calvalcade: Negro American Writing from 1760 to the Present* (with Arthur P. Davis). Boston: Houghton Mifflin, 1971.

## SELECTED PERIODICAL PUBLICATIONS (COMPILED BY PANCHO SAVERY)

"Playing the Numbers." *North American Review* 238 (December 1934): 533–42.

"A Negro Looks at This War." *American Mercury* 55 (November 1942): 585–92.

"A Negro Speaks for His People." *Atlantic Monthly* 171 (March 1943): 58–63.

"The Black Man's Burden." *Antioch Review* 3 (December 1943): 587–95.

"Here's a New Thing Altogether." *Survey Graphic* 33 (August 1944): 358–59.

"The Negro Author: His Publisher, His Public, and His Purse." *Publishers' Weekly* 147 (1945): 1284–1288.

"Portrait: W. E. Burghardt Du Bois." *American Scholar* 18 (January 1949): 93–96.

"American Negro Literature." *American Scholar* 18 (April 1949): 137–48. Rept. in *Afro-American Literature: An Introduction.* Ed. Robert Hayden, David J. Burrows, and Frederick R. Lapides. New York: Harcourt, Brace, Jovanovich, 1971, pp. 273–82.

"The Negro Writer—Shadow and Substance." In "The Negro in Literature: The Current Scene," *Phylon* 2 (1950): 297–374, 371–73.

"No Envy, No Handicap." *Saturday Review* 37 (February 13, 1954): 237.

"Up from Reconstruction." *Nation* 179 (September 4, 1954): 196–97.

"Tonight for Freedom." *American Heritage* 9 (June 1958): 52–55.

"Contradiction de la littérature negro-américaine." *Présence Africaine,* nos. 27–28 (August-November 1959): 11–15.

"The Negro Writer and His Relationship to His Roots." In *The American Negro Writer and His Roots.* New York: American Society of African Culture, 1960, pp. 1–8.

"Negro Writing in America." *New Leader* 42 (May 16, 1960): 8–10.

"In the Vanguard of Civil Rights," *Saturday Review* 44 (August 12, 1961): 34.

"The Alien Land of Richard Wright." In *Soon, One Morning: New Writing by American Negroes, 1940–1962.* Ed. Herbert Hill. New York: Alfred A. Knopf, 1963, pp. 48–59.

"J. S. Redding Talks about African Literature." *AMSAC Newsletter* 5 (September 1962): 1, 4–6.

"Home to Africa." *American Scholar* 32 (Spring 1963): 183–91.

"Sound of Their Masters' Voices." *Saturday Review* 46 (June 29, 1963): 26.

"Modern African Literature." *CLA Journal* 7 (March 1964): 191–201.

"Man against Myth and Malice." *Saturday Review* 47 (May 9, 1964): 48–49.

"The Problems of the Negro Writer." *Massachusetts Review* 6 (Autumn-Winter 1964/5): 57–70.

"The Task of the Negro Writer as Artist: A Symposium." *Negro Digest* 14 (April 1965): 66, 74.

"The Negro Writer and American Literature." In *Anger, and Beyond:*

*The Negro Writer in the United States.* Ed. Herbert Hill. New York: Harper & Row, 1966, pp. 1–19.

(With Herbert Hill, Horace Cayton, and Arna Bontemps): "Reflections on Richard Wright: A Symposium on an Exiled Native Son," In *Anger and Beyond,* pp. 196–212.

"Since Richard Wright." *African Forum* 1 (Spring 1966): 21–31.

"A Survey: Black Writers' Views on Literary Lions and Values." *Negro Digest* 17 (January 1968): 12.

"Literature and the Negro." *Contemporary Literature* 9 (Winter 1968): 130–35.

"Equality and Excellence: The Eternal Dilemma." *William and Mary Review* 6 (Spring 1968): 5–11.

"Of Men and the Writing of Books." Lincoln, Pa.: Vail Memorial Library, Lincoln University, 1969.

"The Negro Writer: The Road Where?" *Boston University Journal* 17 (Winter 1969): 6–10.

"The Black Youth Movement." *American Scholar* 38 (Autumn 1969): 584–87.

"Negro Writing and the Political Climate." Lincoln, Pa.: Vail Memorial Library, Lincoln University, 1970.

"*The Souls of Black Folk:* Du Bois' Masterpiece Lives On." In *Black Titan: W. E. B. Du Bois, An Anthology by the Editors of "Freedomways."* Ed. John Henrik Clarke, Esther Jackson, Ernest Kaiser, and J. H. O'Dell. Boston: Beacon Press, 1970, pp. 47–51.

"The Black Revolution in American Studies." *American Studies: An International Newsletter* 9 (Autumn 1970): 3–9.

"Foreword" to Langston Hughes, *Good Morning Revolution.* Ed. Faith Berry. New York: Lawrence Hill, 1973, pp. ix–x.

"Portrait against Background." In *A Singer in the Dawn: Reinterpretations of Paul Laurence Dunbar.* Ed. Jay Martin. New York: Dodd, Mead, 1975, pp. 39–44.

WORKS ABOUT J. SAUNDERS REDDING

"J. Saunders Redding." *Twentieth Century Authors* (First Supplement, 1955).

"J. Saunders Redding." *Contemporary Authors,* vol. IV (1963).

"J. Saunders Redding." *Who's Who in America, 1968–69.*

"(Jay) Saunders Redding." *Current Biography, 1969,* pp. 356–57.

Davis, Arthur P. "Saunders Redding." *From the Dark Tower.* Washington, D.C.: Howard University Press, 1973, pp. 157–61.

"J. Saunders Redding." *Encyclopedia of Black America.* Ed. W. Augustus Low and Virgil A. Clift (1981), p. 728.

Stiles, Martin B. "Fellowships for Minorities Will Honor J. Saunders Redding." *Cornell Chronicle,* May 29, 1986, p. 3.

Williams, Dennis A. "An Integrating Voice." *Cornell Alumni News* 89 (December 1986): 22–25.

Savery, Pancho. "J. Saunders Redding." *The Dictionary of American Literary Biography: American Literary Critics.* In press.

# Preface

It has long seemed important to bring together certain factual material and critical opinion on American Negro literature in a sort of history of Negro thought in America. A quarter of a century ago the task would have been considered a waste of time, for the material (and this combined with its relative paucity) was thought to have little bearing upon the general tide of American life. Even the profound influence of the spirituals and other folk matter upon native culture was not fully realized. But change came: the interest of both scholars and laymen was aroused. In the past few years many things have combined to reveal the importance of literary development among Negroes since Jupiter Hammon.

Today no one who studies even superficially the history of the Negro in America can fail to see the uncommon relationship of his letters to that history; nor can one fail to remark that literary expression for the Negro has not been, and is not wholly now an art in the sense that the poetry and prose of another people, say the Irish, is art. Almost from the very beginning the literature of the Negro has been literature either of purpose or necessity, and it is because of this that it appeals as much to the cognitive as to the conative and affective side of man's being. The study of the literature of these dark Americans becomes, therefore, a practical, as opposed to a purely speculative, exercise.

What results are obtained from such a study, it is the purpose of this book to indicate. No apology is offered for excluding certain writers whose work, well thought of, simply has no bearing upon the important trends and developments either of thought or forms of expression. The material of an ordinary history of Negro literature is thus cut more than half. Though written with a mind for the problems of students, it is hoped that the "odor of scholarship" attaches to it so slightly as to give the book some appeal to popular taste; for ultimately literature, if it is to live at all, must be in the strictest sense popular.

# Acknowledgments

The author gratefully acknowledges permission from the following persons and firms to reprint from material controlled by them:
Dodd, Mead & Company (Various selections from *The Complete Poems of Paul Laurence Dunbar.* Used by permission of the publishers, Dodd, Mead & Company, Inc.). Harcourt, Brace & Company ("If We Must Die" and "The Tropics in New York" from *Harlem Shadows*, by Claude McKay; "Litany of Atlanta," "Credo," and "The Riddle of the Sphinx" from *Darkwater*, by W. E. B. DuBois; "Memphis Blues," "Strange Legacies," and the Preface, from *Southern Road*, by Sterling A. Brown). Harper & Brothers ("To Certain Critics" from *The Black Christ;* "Foreword" from *Caroling Dusk;* "Yet Do I Marvel," "Incident," and "To My Fairer Brethren" from *Color;* a short selection from the jacket of *Copper Sun*—all by Countee Cullen). Alfred A. Knopf, Inc. ("Negro Dancers" from *Weary Blues* and "Afraid" from *Fine Clothes to the Jew*, by Langston Hughes, by permission of and special arrangement with Alfred A. Knopf, Inc., authorized publishers). Liveright Publishing Corporation ("Song of the Son" and "Georgia Dusk" from *Cane*, by Jean Toomer, published by Liveright Publishing Corp.). A. C. McClurg & Company and the author (Various selections from *The Souls Of Black Folk*, by W. E. B. DuBois). Frederick A. Stokes Company (An excerpt from *The Chinaberry Tree*, by Jessie Fauset). The Stratford Company and the author ("My Race" from *Wings of Oppression*, by Leslie Pinckney Hill). Viking Press, Inc. ("Lift Every Voice and Sing," "Fifty Years," "Sence You Went Away," and "My City" from *Saint Peter Relates an Incident*, by James Weldon Johnson.

# CONTENTS

# TO MAKE A POET BLACK

Inscrutable His ways are and immune
To catechism by a mind too strewn
With petty cares to slightly understand
What awful brain compels His awful hand ;
Yet do I marvel at this curious thing :
To make a poet black, and bid him sing!

—*Countee Cullen*

# 1. The Forerunners

JUPITER HAMMON, PHILLIS WHEATLEY, GEORGE MOSES
HORTON

§ 1

The literature of the Negro in America, motivated as it is by his very practical desire to adjust himself to the American environment, is "literature of necessity." Until recent years the Negro writer has not known what it is to write without this motivation, and even now, of the dozens of writers who have published in the last twenty years the work of but two seems wholly independent of this influence. At the very heart of this literature, then, lies the spore of a cankerous growth. This might be said to be the necessity of ends. But there is also a necessity of means. Negro writers have been obliged to have two faces. If they wished to succeed they have been obliged to satisfy two different (and opposed when not entirely opposite) audiences, the black and the white. This necessity of means, perhaps, has been even stronger than the necessity of ends, and as writers have increased, the necessity has grown almost to the point of desperation.

From Jupiter Hammon, the first Negro writer in America, to Countee Cullen and Langston Hughes, these two necessities can be traced with varying degrees of clarity—now one and now the other predominant—like threads through the whole cloth. With the very earliest writers the needs did not encompass more than personal self, but as consciousness of others awakened in later writers and as the simplicity of the Negro's primary position in America changed successively to the complexity of the times of abolition agitation, freedom, enfranchisement, and social self-determination the artless personality of his literature dropped away and he became the sometimes frenzied propagandist of racial consciousness and advancement.

§ 2

Jupiter Hammon was the first American Negro to see his name in print as a maker of verse. The date of his birth is uncertain, but the earliest reference to him is found in a letter dated May 19, 1730, when he was probably a little more than ten years old.[1] At this time he was the slave of Henry Lloyd of Queens Village, Long Island. The date of his death is likewise uncertain, but was very probably not earlier than 1806.

Hammon's first published work was "An Evening Thought: Salvation by Christ, with Penetential Cries" in 1760. His next work, "A Poetical Address to Phillis Wheatley," was published eighteen years later, but it is improbable that the intervening years were devoid of literary activity, especially considering that Hammon was something of a preacher among his people, a fact which plainly had a bearing upon his work. "An Essay on the Ten Virgins," of which no copy is extant, was printed in 1779. In 1782 he published "A Winter Piece" with "A Poem for Children with Thoughts on Death" and "An Evening's Improvement" to which was appended a rhymed dialogue entitled "The Kind Master and Dutiful Servant." The last of his printed work, "An Address to Negroes in the State of New York," was issued in 1787 and reached three editions.

Hammon was an intelligent and privileged slave, respected by the master class for his skill with tools and by the slaves for his power as a preacher. His verse is rhymed prose, doggerel, in which the homely thoughts of a very religious and superstitious man are expressed in limping phrases. Now and then his lines have a lyric swing that

seems to mark them as having been chanted spontaneously
in the sermons he preached. Undoubtedly some lines from
"An Evening Thought" have this lyric significance. The
alternately rhyming lines lend themselves very easily and
nicely to religious chanting.

Salvation comes by Christ alone,
The only son of God;
Redemption now to every one,
That love his holy word.

Dear Jesus unto Thee we cry,
Give us the preparation;
Turn not away thy tender eye;
We seek thy true salvation.

Of the work of this kind, the piece addressed to Phillis
Wheatley is the best. Hammon must have struck responsive
chords in the breast of the young Massachusetts slave who
already at this time had been acclaimed in England as an
unusual poet. Both were extremely religious, and both pre-
ferred slavery in America to freedom in Africa. Each of the
twenty-one quatrains of "The Address to Phillis Wheatley"
has a marginal note of reference to the Bible.

I

O come you pious youth! Adore
The wisdom of thy God,
In bringing thee from distant shore
To learn his holy word.

II

Thou mightst been left behind,
Amidst a dark abode;

God's tender mercy still combin'd,
Thou hast the holy word.

IV

God's tender mercy brought thee here;
Tost o'er the raging main;
In Christian faith thou hast a share,
Worth all the gold of Spain.

IX

Come you, Phillis, now aspire,
And seek the living God,
So step by step thou mayest go higher,
Till perfect in the word.

Almost did Miss Wheatley express Hammon's exact thought
in her lines "To The University of Cambridge."

'T was not long since I left my native shore,
The land of errors and Egyptian gloom:
Father of mercy! 't was thy gracious hand
Brought me in safety from those dark abodes.

On the whole, Hammon's untutored art offered but narrow scope for the fullest expression. His most substantial
contribution to Negro literature prior to the Civil War is in
prose, and whatever of literary merit he possessed must be
looked for in his single prose piece, "An Address to the
Negroes in the State of New York." This work reveals more
of Hammon's workaday character than all his poetry together. The thoughts expressed in "An Address to Negroes"
are not typical of the thoughts of slaves, especially those who
were unfortunate enough to have had some education. With
the notable exception of Phillis Wheatley, the slave writers

were bitterly reproachful of bondage. Many slaves who could neither read nor write but who were nonetheless truly poetic burned themselves out in revolt. To the splendid folly of their deeds Hammon's equivocal statement is an outrage. A summation of his philosophy and a clear-cut statement of his resignation to a life of servitude is found in his words :

"Respecting obedience to masters. Now whether it is right and lawful in the sight of God, for them to make slaves of us or not, I am certain that while we are slaves, it is our duty to obey our masters in all their lawful commands, and mind them. . . . As we depend upon our masters for what we eat and drink and wear, we cannot be happy unless we obey them."[2]

Hammon's life was motivated by the compulsion of obedience to his earthly and his heavenly master. Perhaps the inevitability of his position tended to wilt his moral fiber. Perhaps the beneficence of his masters lightened the burden of his bondage. Though he was the first Negro slave to publish an adverse opinion on the institution of slavery, his opinion was robbed of its force by the words "though for my own part I do not wish to be free." Perhaps it was the very weakness of the statement that recommended it for publication. At the same time, however, his hedging was not without its wisdom. He says :

"Now I acknowledge that liberty is a great thing, and worth seeking for, if we can get it honestly; and by our good conduct prevail upon our masters to set us free : though for my own part I do not wish to be free, yet I should be glad if others, especially the young negroes, were to be free ; for many of us who are grown up slaves, and have always had masters to take care of us, should hardly know how to take care of themselves. . . . That liberty is a great thing we may know from our own feelings, and we may likewise judge so from the conduct of the white people in the late war.

How much money has been spent and how many lives have been lost to defend their liberty! I must say that I have hoped that God would open their eyes, when they were so much engaged for liberty, to think of the state of the poor blacks, and to pity us."[3]

As to literary values, there is not much to choose between Hammon's poetry and prose. Though he was not without the romantic gift of spontaneity, he lacked any knowledge of metrics and sought only to make rhymes. In prose the artlessness of his construction, the rambling sentences, the repetitions reveal, sometimes at the expense of thought, his not unattractive personality. When he is most lucid there is force in the quaintness of his thought evocative of the highly personal flavor of early American letters.

§ 3

Little more is known of the birth of Phillis Wheatley than of Jupiter Hammon. At the time of her purchase by John Wheatley in 1761 she was judged to be in her seventh or eighth year from "the circumstance of shedding her front teeth." She was a scrawny child, alert with the precocity so often associated with physical frailty. Mrs. Wheatley was quick to realize Phillis's unusual intelligence, but she could not possibly tell that this little slave girl, scarcely more than a useless luxury at first, was to become in England the best-known of contemporary American poets.

Phillis's life with the Wheatleys was in every way exceptional. Taught to read and write, nurtured and tutored with the greatest care, within a year and a half of her arrival from Africa she had acquired a sufficient command of the English language "to read any, the most difficult parts of the sacred writings." Two years later she had written her first poems.

There is no question but that Miss Wheatley considered

herself a Negro poet: the question is to what degree she felt the full significance of such a designation. Certainly she was not a *slave* poet in any sense in which the term can be applied to many who followed her. She stood far outside the institution that was responsible for her. As for the question of degree, though she refers to herself time and again as an "Ethiop," she seems to make such reference with a distinct sense of abnegation and self-pity.

> Father of mercy! 'T was thy gracious hand
> Brought me in safety from those dark abodes.

This attitude on the part of Miss Wheatley was the result of the training and conduct of her life. Treated as one of the Wheatley family on terms of almost perfect equality, petted and made much of, she was sagacious enough to see that this was due in part at least to her exotic character and sensitive enough to feel that her color was really a bar to a more desirable, if less flattering, attention. At best this life was not too dear to Phillis. She recounts the joys of the life to come in the strains of one who looks upon this life as though it were a strange and bitter preparation for an eternity of bliss. The Wheatleys had adopted her, but she had adopted their terrific New England conscience. Her conception of the after-life was different from that of most of the slaves as we find it expressed in songs and spirituals. No contemplation of physical luxuries of feastings, jeweled crowns, and snowy robes enticed her. Her heaven must be a place of the purest sublimation of spirit. Less than this would serve but to remind her of this dark bourne of flesh and blood.

But if the degree to which she felt herself a Negro poet was slight, the extent to which she was attached spiritually and emotionally to the slaves is even slighter. By 1761 slavery was an important almost daily topic. The Boston home of the Wheatleys, intelligent and alive as it was, could not have been deaf to the discussions of restricting the slave trade, especially since by 1770 Massachusetts, Pennsylvania, and Virginia had each taken steps in that direction. Nothing so hard and definite as the abolition movement had been put forward, but when Miss Wheatley landed in England in 1773 freedom was a vital topic in pulpit and Parliament. Not once, however, did she express in either word or action a thought on the enslavement of her race; not once did she utter a straightforward word for the freedom of the Negro. When she did speak of freedom in a letter to the Earl of Dartmouth, it was:

> No more, America, in mournful strain,
> Of wrongs and grievances unredressed complain;
> No longer shall thou dread the iron chain
> Which wanton Tyranny with lawless hand,
> Had made, and with it meant t' enslave the land.

Toward the end of this poetic epistle she says the only thing that may be taken as an indictment of human slavery. Yet even in these lines the effect is vitiated.

> Should you, my lord, while you peruse my song,
> Wonder from whence my love of freedom sprung,
> Whence flow these wishes for the common good,
> By feeling hearts alone best understood,
> I, young in life, by seeming cruel fate
> Was snatched from Afric's fancied happy seat.[4]

"Seeming cruel" and "fancied happy" give her away as not believing either in the cruelty of the fate that had dragged thousands of her race into bondage in America nor in the happiness of their former freedom in Africa. How different the spirit of her work, and how unracial (not to say unnatural) are the stimuli that release her wan creative energies. How different are these from the work of George Horton who twenty-five years later could cry out with bitterness, without cavil or fear :

> Alas! and am I born for this,
> To wear this slavish chain?[5]

It is this negative, bloodless, unracial quality in Phillis Wheatley that makes her seem superficial, especially to members of her own race. Hers is a spirit-denying-the-flesh attitude that somehow cannot seem altogether real as the essential quality and core of one whose life should have made her sensitive to the very things she denies. In this sense none of her poetry is real. Compared to the Negro writers who followed her, Miss Wheatley's passions are tame, her skill the sedulous copy of established techniques, and her thoughts the hand-me-downs of her age. She is chilly. Part of her chill is due to the unmistakable influence of Pope's neoclassicism upon her. She followed the fashion in poetry. Overemphasis of religion was a common fault of the time. She indulged it in poetic epistles, eulogistic verse, verses written in praise of accomplishments. Her ready submission to established forms was a weakness of the period. First and last, she was the fragile product of three related forces—the age, the Wheatley household, and New England America. Her work lacks spontaneity because of the first, enthusiasm because of the second, and because of the third it lacks an unselfish purpose that drives to some ultimate goal of expression.

And yet she had poetic talent, was in fact a poet. No one who reads the following lines from "Thoughts on the Works of Providence" can deny it.

> Infinite love, where'r we turn our eyes,
> Appears : this ev'ry creatures want supplies ;
> This most is heard in nature's constant voice ;
> This makes the morn, and this the eve, rejoice ;
> This bids the fostering rains and dews descend
> To nourish all, to serve one gen'ral end,
> The good of man : yet man ungrateful pays
> But little homage, and but little praise.
> To Him whose works arrayed in mercy shine,
> What songs should rise, how constant, how divine![6]

Judged in the light of the day in which she wrote, judged by that day's standards and accomplishments, she was an important poet. As a Negro poet she stands out remarkably, for her work lacks the characteristics of thought one would expect to find. She was the first Negro woman in America to write and publish poetry.

The story of her life following her return from England is soon told by the anonymous writer of the *Memoirs of Phillis Wheatley*. Her health, never sound, grew precarious. In 1778 she married a Negro doctor, lawyer, and groceryman named John Peters, by whom she had two children. Peters proved worthless, deserting her in her utmost need, when the older Wheatleys were dead and the younger ones scattered.

"In a filthy apartment, in an obscure part of the metropolis, lay the dying mother and child. The woman who had stood honored and respected by the wise and good in that country which was hers by adoption, or rather compulsion, who had graced the ancient halls of old England, and had rolled about in the splendid equipages of the proud nobles

of Britain, was now numbering the last hours of her life in
a state of the most abject misery, surrounded by all the
emblems of squalid poverty. . . .

"The friends of Phillis who had visited her in her sickness,
knew not of her death. . . . A grand-niece of Phillis's bene-
factress, passing up Court street, met the funeral of an adult
and a child : a by-stander informed her that they were bearing Phillis to that silent mansion."[7]

## § 4

What Hammon lacked in audacity and color and what
Miss Wheatley failed to show in enthusiasm and racial kinship is more than supplied by George Moses Horton. If the
former were motivated only by an aimless urge to write,
finding as they went along, willy-nilly, ideas, emotions, and
thoughts to give expression to, Horton started from an emotional basis. He first wanted to say something. Hammon
and Miss Wheatley were negative ; Horton was positive. He
felt, albeit selfishly, the motivation derived from the Negro's
position in America. He felt, too, something of the wonder
and mystery, the tragic beauty, and the pathetic ugliness of
life. Above all, he had the gift of laughter. He was the first
"natural-born" poet of the Negro race in America.

Horton was born a slave in North Carolina about the year
1797. The exact date is uncertain. At a reception given him
in Philadelphia in 1866, he was said to have remarked that
his former master reckoned his age by looking into his mouth,
judged the state of his health by whipping him, and deter-
mined the condition of his immortal soul by damning him
to hell. Horton was an incorrigible actor and laugh-baiter,
never missing an opportunity (at the cost of no matter what
falsehood) to dramatize himself. When his first volume,
*Hope of Liberty*, was published in 1829, Weston R. Gales,
editor of the *Raleigh Register* and one of the men interested

in helping Horton gain his freedom, judged him to be about thirty-two years old.

Though Horton very soon gave evidence of hating slavery, it does not seem that he was more than nominally restrained by his slave status. What Horton's occupations and wanderings were we do not know, but he gained somehow considerably more knowledge of the world than fell to the lot of most slaves. By the 1820's he had become known in Raleigh and was probably at that time working around the State University at Chapel Hill and writing for students the poems that made him something of a campus celebrity.

The poems of this period are not available, but they must have been light and more or less humorously concerned with love, the sort of jingles that would delight young college students. Certainly it is inconceivable that the provincial sons of the South, many of them slaveholders, would have paid the poet for poems in which he railed against slavery. Indeed it may be that at this time Horton's feelings about slavery had not crystallized into hatred. It seems fair to judge these earlier poems, then, by later work of the same kind.

Later Horton learned to hate. Perhaps his disappointment over his failure to purchase his freedom had something to do with it. As early as 1822 he had had elaborate dreams of migrating to the free colony of Liberia. Perhaps from the North there had drifted down to him some word of the sympathetic interest his scattered poems had created. At any rate, he was fully aware of the desirability of a life of freedom. Though only three poems on slavery appeared in *Hope of Liberty*, one is inclined to the belief that "some of the poems deleted in the interest of the author" were of this nature. Since the volume was manifestly published to obtain funds with which to purchase Horton's freedom, this seems all the more likely.

Though throughout the book he shows a consistently good and original nature, dwelling much on religion, nature, and love, now and then he expresses the dark bitterness with which his lot afflicted him. From the hopeful hymn that opens the volume,

> Creation fires my tongue!
> Nature, thy anthems raise;
> And spread the universal song
> Of thy Creator's praise!

he could come to the following lament, the meter of which was certainly inspired by the Methodist hymns with which he was familiar:

> Alas! and am I born for this,
>     To wear this slavish chain?
> Deprived of all created bliss,
>     Through hardship, toil, and pain?
>
> How long have I in bondage lain,
>     And languished to be free!
> Alas! and must I still complain,
>     Deprived of liberty?[8]

The financial purpose of the book failed, and from 1829 on there is increasing evidence that Horton "played" his misfortunes, real or imaginary, "to the grandstand." It is not known who inspired the editor's hint in the preface to the Philadelphia edition of *Hope of Liberty* (1837) that Weston Gales had retained the money realized from the Raleigh printing, but an impartial judgment of Horton's later character makes one believe it was likely Horton himself. Naïvely selfish and stuffed with the vanity of a child, his conduct after his escape to Philadelphia and freedom toward the close of the civil struggle was said to have been unbearable. The free Negroes, of which at the time there were considerable numbers in Philadelphia, could not tolerate his demeanor, the childish strutting that had made him a character in the South. After a few weeks, they dropped him so completely that John Hawkins, who was a boy of thirteen in 1880, and whose parents knew Horton well, could not recall when or where the poet died.

Though Horton fully realized the bitterness of bondage, he tasted its gall only for himself. He seems to have thought that slavery was created for himself alone. In this he differs from Miss Wheatley in that she seemed never fully to appreciate her slave status. If she was not aroused by it for others, neither was she aroused by it for herself. Horton, wholly aware, satisfied himself with but one expressed thought for others:

> Love which can ransom every slave,
>     And set the pris'ner free;
> Gild the dark horrors of the grave,
>     And still the raging sea.[9]

Even later, when the *New York Tribune*, probably America's greatest paper at that time, began to publish antislavery sentiment and the editor, Horace Greeley, became interested in Horton, it was the same. The best that Horton could attain was a conceited plea for his own deliverance:

> Let me no longer be a slave,
>     But drop the fetters and be free.
>
> .     .     .     .     .
>
> Oh, listen all who never felt
>     For fettered genius heretofore,

Let hearts of petrification melt,
And bid the gifted negro soar.[10]

After 1837 various of Horton's poems appeared in northern periodicals of abolitionist leanings or declaration, like the *North Star*, Frederick Douglass's Rochester paper, the *Liberator*, and the *Lancaster* (Pa.) *Gazette*. In 1838, George Light published in Boston an edition of Horton's *Hope of Liberty* and bound it with the memoir and poems of Phillis Wheatley. The full title of this edition was, *Memoir and Poems of Phillis Wheatley, a Native African and Slave: Also, Poems by a Slave*. In 1865 there was printed at Raleigh the second and final volume of Horton's poems, *Naked Genius*, which seems to contain a great many earlier poems not published before.

Between 1829 and 1865 Horton seems not to have grown at all, though the later pieces in *Naked Genius* reveal a return of that good humor that helped the sale of his earlier poems to the university students. He never lost his naïve conceit. His poems are concerned with love and nature, heavenly grace and divine miracles. Remarkable among his characteristics is his imagery, generally as confused and wasteful and rich as a tropic sunset, but sometimes astonishingly fine and telling.

'T was like fair Helen's sweet return to Troy.[11]

At his command the water blushed
And all was turned to wine.[12]

Remarkable, too, are the turns of humor which deny the simplicity of his mind and character. It is unfortunate that so much of his Chapel Hill verse was lost, for in those days of his youth the humor must have been much more audacious and sparkling, though perhaps less sophistical. It may be that those early verses are an important loss to American humor. The finger-snapping flippancy of "Jeff Davis in a Tight Place" and "Creditor to His Proud Debtor" are not unworthy of a Holmes.

> My duck bill boots would look as bright,
> Had you in justice served me right;
> Like you, I then could step as light,
>     Before a flaunting maid.
> As nicely could I clear my throat,
> And to my tights my eyes devote;
> But I'd leave you bare, without the coat
>     For which you have not paid.
>
> Then boast and bear the crack,
> With the sheriff at your back,
> Huzzah for dandy Jack,
> My jolly fop, my Jo![13]

Beside the gray-mantled figures of Hammon and Phillis Wheatley, Horton appears dressed in motley. His humor, his audacious and homely wit, his lack of dignity give him important historical place as the forerunner of the minstrel poets, and this consideration outweighs whatever of intrinsic poetical value his poems possess.

# 2. Let Freedom Ring

CHARLES REMOND, WILLIAM W. BROWN, FREDERICK
DOUGLASS, FRANCES ELLEN WATKINS, JAMES MADISON
BELL

§ 1

Through the years from the middle 1700's onward, hundreds
of slaves escaped by various means (notably the Under-
ground Railroad) into free territory. By 1810 there were
78,011 free Negroes in the United States. Some of these had
never been slaves, in fact owned slaves themselves, and
others had gained freedom through manumission. A great
many of them, finding a more or less satisfactory existence
in the South, felt no desire or need for expression in other
than the ways conventionally attributed to the Negro of
that era. They went to camp meetings and picnics, baptisms
and revivals, where they gave themselves over to the singing of glory songs and work songs, the chanting of spirituals
and the moaning of prayers. The spirituals and prayers, the
sermons and work songs which survive from this great body
of folk literature testify to the adequacy of their emotional
and imaginative release. But with the freeman, the freedman, and the escaped slave in the North, matters were vastly
different. Among them had come as refugees in 1793 a
number of Santo Domingo Negroes from whom they learned
the revolutionary doctrines of the French. Some of the more
advanced of the northern Negroes were formally educated,
and most of them were intelligent enough to wish to live
normal and prosperous lives in the free communities of the
North. They were bound together in an economic and racial
struggle to a degree unknown to their brothers in the South.

These people soon felt the need for racial expression, and
the white friends of freedom in the North, especially in

western New York State and Boston, gave them their opportunity. The various antislavery groups, combining their
efforts under the American Convention of Abolition Society,
planned a definite and effective campaign of propaganda
in which the more intelligent free and escaped Negroes were
to play a large part. As early as 1831 attempts had been
made by proponents of slavery to connect William Lloyd
Garrison with slave insurrections in the South, for it was
known that he was an avowed friend to David Walker, the
Negro author of the famous *Appeal* of 1829 and a man who
had published his intention to lead an insurrection.[1] In the
same year (1831) Garrison founded the *Liberator* in Boston,
and immediately the Negro recognized the voice of a champion raised in his behalf. The first Negro magazine, *The
African Methodist Episcopal Magazine*, appeared in 1841 as the
official organ of a new religious body, the African Methodist
Episcopal Church. In 1848 Frederick Douglass's paper, the
*North Star*, was founded in Rochester, New York. Besides
these there were the abolitionist papers, the *Anti-Slavery
Standard*, the *Herald of Freedom*, and the *Anti-Slavery Bugle*,
and there were "numerous attempts at poetical composition,
and several booklets were published."[2]

Despite these media for racial expression, the literature
of the Negro in the North (as of his brother in the South)
was at this time essentially an oral literature. All over the
faction-torn nation oratory was considered the final accomplishment of accomplished men. Negroes learned quickly
from such polished platform speakers as Wendell Phillips,
William Lloyd Garrison, Charles Sumner, and Stephen
Douglas. The two decades before the Civil War, the war
period itself, and the years immediately following saw the
rise of such exponents of the art of oratory as Charles Remond, William Wells Brown, Lunsford Lane, Sojourner
Truth, David Walker, and Frederick Douglass, men and

women whose voices were often heard across the Atlantic, where some of them went as speakers for the American Anti-Slavery Society. Some of these, it is true, did some writing, and William Brown was for a time a regular contributor to the *London Daily News*. Besides this, he had seven volumes to his credit, including a drama and a novel. The autobiographies of Frederick Douglass and Samuel Ward were quite popular, while David Walker's *Appeal*, published in September 1829, had run to three editions by March 1830.

But this does not alter the fact that the more than half century from 1830 to 1895 was for the Negro a period of spoken prose literature of protest. As speakers in the ranks of the abolitionists many Negro men and women helped develop the spoken literature, but most of these merely filled the need of the day, passing out of memory when the need was no longer. Three men remain as most representative of the temper and opinion of the Negro in those years.

Of the three, Charles Remond, William Wells Brown, and Frederick Douglass, Remond is the only one who did not leave behind him an autobiography. From Remond's speeches one gathers that he was born free, a fact that so influenced him that he felt more keenly the prejudice against his class than he did the social evil of slavery. A great many of his speeches are concerned less with exhorting for abolition than with bringing about a desired change in the attitude of the whites toward the free people of color. For thirty years he was engaged as a lecturer by the Anti-Slavery Society. In 1840 he was sent to England as a delegate to the World Anti-Slavery Society convention. Abroad until 1842, his speeches gained him considerable attention. Because his oratory was essentially an oratory of fine language, today doubtless he would be thought too smooth, too suave in speech and manner. Nevertheless his record between 1830

and 1860 is a substantial one, marred only by the jealous
attacks he made upon Frederick Douglass.

Even for those days of momentous social change Remond
was radical. An extract from a speech delivered to the New
England Anti-Slavery convention of 1859 shows him at his
best:

"If I had but one reason why I consented to appear here,
it was because, at this moment, I believe it belongs to the
colored man in this country to say that his lot is a common
one with every white man north of the Potomac river. . . .

"The time has been, Mr. Chairman, when a colored man
could scarcely look a white man in the face without trem-
bling, owing to his education and experience. I am not here
to boast; but I may say, in view of what I have seen and
heard during the last five years, as I said in the Representatives Hall a few months ago, that our lot is a common
one and the sooner we shall regard it so and buckle on our
knapsacks and shoulder our muskets, and resolve that we
will be free, the better for you as well as for me. The disgrace
that once rested upon the head of the black man, now hovers
over the head of every man and woman whom I have the
honor to address this evening, just in proportion as they
shall dare to stand erect before the oligarchy of slaveholders
in the Southern part of the country; and God hasten forward the day when not only Music Hall, but every other
hall in the city of Boston, the Athens of America, shall be
made eloquent with tones that shall speak as man has never
spoken before in this country, for the cause of universal
freedom. If the result of that speaking must be bloodshed,
be it so! If it must be the dissolution of the Union, be it so!
The time has come when if you value your own freedom,
James Buchanan must be hung in effigy, and such men as
Nehemiah Adams must be put in pillory of public disgrace

and contempt; and thus Massachusetts will cease to be a hissing and a byword in every country."[3]

## § 2

The most unusual figure in the literary history of the American Negro is William Wells Brown. A great deal of the interest which attaches to him is, perhaps, artificial, growing out of the confusion and variety of the stories he told about himself. At one time or another he put forward at least three versions of his parentage and early childhood. In what seems to be the first autobiographical account, he tells us that he was born in Kentucky of slave parents, and that as a child he learned to work in the field and in the house. In the second account he sheds no further light on his ancestry, but tells us that he was stolen by a slave trader shortly after birth. Finally, in the second revised edition of his *Narrative*, he divulges that he was born on an undetermined date in Lexington, Kentucky, of a white father (scion of the family to which his mother was slave) and a mother whose father, "it was said, was the noted Daniel Boone." All accounts agree on two circumstances: that he was born in Kentucky, and that later, while still a boy, he escaped into Ohio.

The discrepancies in the stories of Brown's birth and his early life may be due to one of three things: Brown himself may have been untruthful; unscrupulous publishers, seeking to dress an old tale in more attractive colors, may have been responsible; and last, the white-father, Daniel Boone-grandfather version may have been invented by abolitionist editors in an effort further to stigmatize slavery. White (and generally aristocratic) paternity was certainly a favorite propagandic device in the fictional stories of slaves. It was used to show the demoralizing effect of slavery upon the master class. Many so-called biographies and autobiographies of "escaped slaves" were pure inventions of white writers of the period.

When Brown escaped into Ohio he was befriended by a Quaker, Wells Brown, from whom he took his name. Later he seems to have been recaptured, and through various changes in his ownership he became a cabin boy on the Mississippi, a confidential assistant to a slave trader, and finally a printer's devil in (and this is his own unestablished story) the news office of Elijah P. Lovejoy, an abolitionist journalist in St. Louis who was later killed for his liberal views. Brown tells us that it was in his capacity as printer's devil that he learned to read. Later he went into Canada.

Brown earned his living as he could and spent most of his spare time in study. Certainly in western New York State, to which he eventually made his way, there was abroad enough of the spirit of freedom and democracy to encourage him. An impressionable man all his life, he was touched by nearly everything he heard and saw, absorbing much that was odd and valueless along with that that was solid and worthwhile. His autobiographies are full of his early impressions as an escaped slave. Finally, "impressed with the importance of spreading anti-slavery truth, as a means of abolishing slavery, I commenced lecturing as an agent of the western New York Anti-Slavery Society, and have ever since devoted my time to the cause of my enslaved countrymen." Though this work engaged him for fifteen years, and though it has been estimated that he delivered in England alone a thousand speeches during a stay of five years from 1849 to 1854, Brown's speeches are lost for the most part. This apparently studied neglect of his own speeches seems to indicate that he was interested chiefly in writing.

William Wells Brown was the first serious creative prose

writer of the Negro race in America. Three editions of the *Narrative of William Wells Brown*, his first considerable work, appeared under the sponsorship of the Massachusetts Anti-Slavery Society between 1847 and 1849. *The Black Man, St. Domingo*, and *Three Years In Europe* were published before the close of the Civil War, and though the first two of these were attempts at objective historical writing and the third was a travel account, Brown was so dominated by "the cause of my countrymen" that his facts are garbled to serve the ends of propaganda.

When the slavery controversy had settled into well-defined patterns and the cause for which he had begun his career was no longer so pressing, Brown launched his purely imaginative efforts. This period from about 1850 to 1865 was productive of two novels, *Clotel; or The President's Daughter* (1853) and *Miralda; or The Beautiful Quadroon* (1867) and a play, *The Escape* (1858). These are the first pieces of fiction and the first play by an American Negro. After the war Brown did his more reasonable and most ambitious works, two histories and a group of narrative essays. *The Negro in the American Rebellion* was published in 1868, *The Rising Son* in 1874, and *My Southern Home* in 1880.

In facility of expression, in artistic discrimination, and in narrative skill Brown advanced steadily from the *Narrative* to the essays which comprise his last work. Historically more important in the development of Negro literature than any of his contemporaries, he was also the most representative Negro of the age, for he was simply a man of slightly more than ordinary talents doing his best in a cause that was his religion. Frederick Douglass was too exceptional; Remond too selfish. Almost without forethought, like an inspired prophet, Brown gave expression to the hope and despair, the thoughts and yearnings of thousands of what he was pleased to call his "countrymen."

Brown had the vital energy that is part of the equipment of all artists. He wrote with force, with clarity, and at times with beauty. There is in his work, however, a repetitious amplification that is not altogether accountable to a desire for perfection. His autobiography, first published in 1847, had been spun out to twice its original length by the time of its publication in London two years later. *St. Domingo*, originally a speech and later a pamphlet, finally became the basis for several chapters on the West Indies in *The Rising Son*. Certain episodes from his *Narrative* were used as starting points for pieces in *My Southern Home*. *Three Years in Europe* came to America as *Sketches of Places and People Abroad*. *Clotel* was attenuated (by deleting the unseen antagonist, Thomas Jefferson, and by making various lengthening changes) into *Clotelle; a Tale of the Southern States*. If Brown's play, *Dough-face*, mentioned by William Simmons,[4] ever comes to light, it is likely that it will be found to be merely an earlier sketch of the drama, *The Escape, or A Leap for Freedom*, published in 1858 and read in many parts of the country prior to that. Even *Miralda* got mixed up with *Clotel*, but this time it was *Clotelle, The Colored Heroine*.

Brown was driven by the necessity for turning out propaganda in a cause that was too close to him for emotional objectivity and reasonable perspective. He had power without the artist's control, but in spite of this his successes are considerable and of great importance to the history of Negro creative literature. First novelist, first playwright, first historian: the list argues his place. It is doubtful that in the writing of his novels, plays, and histories he saw beyond "the cause." Even in the later years of his life, when it seems he would have been free to focus artistically, he did not change too appreciably. *The Rising Son*, done with an eye to fact, to cause and effect, and to arriving at logical conclusions, is undoubtedly an advance over *The Black Man*, but it is also a deliberate plea in behalf of the Negro race. *My Southern Home* is a vastly better book than the *Narrative*, but less in the sense of artistic objectivity than in craftsmanship. All his days Brown was first a Negro and then a writer.

At its best Brown's language is cursive and strong, adapted to the treatment he gives his material. When he held his bitterness in check, he was inclined to lay on a heavy coating of sentimental morality. Often his lack of control did hurt to an otherwise good passage. A slave-auction scene in *Clotel* illustrates his fault. After a racy and realistic description of a Richmond slave market in which a beautiful quadroon girl was struck off to the highest bidder, Brown ends thus : "This was a Virginia slave-auction, at which the bones, sinews, blood and nerves of a young girl of eighteen were sold for $500 : her moral character for $200 ; her superior intellect for $100 ; the benefits supposed to accrue from her having been sprinkled and immersed, together with a warranty of her devoted christianity, for $300 ; her ability to make a good prayer for $200 ; and her chastity for $700 more. This, too, in a city thronged with churches, whose tall spires look like so many signals pointing to heaven, but whose ministers preach that slavery is a God-ordained institution."

Though it is possible that Brown was true to fact in the following passage, there is nevertheless a loss of force. This loss is due to his failure to see *truth* beyond mere fact. It may be that his mother did talk and act as he has her talk and act in the following passage of the *Narrative*, but she is not real to us either as an individual or a type.

"At about ten o'clock in the morning I went on board the boat and found her there in company with fifty or sixty other slaves. She was chained to another woman. On seeing me, she immediately dropped her head on her heaving bosom. She moved not, neither did she weep. Her emotions were too deep for tears. I approached, threw my arms around her neck, kissed her, and fell upon my knees, begging her forgiveness, for I thought myself to blame for her sad condition. . . .

"She finally raised her head, looked me in the face, (and such a look none but an angel can give!) and said, 'My dear son, you are not to blame for my being here. You have done nothing more nor less than your duty. Do not, I pray you, weep for me. I cannot last long upon a cotton plantation. I feel that my heavenly master will soon call me home, and then I shall be out of the hands of the slaveholders!' "

Like many of Brown's shortcomings, the fault of sacrificing truth to fact is the result of the necessity of yielding to the demands of propaganda. He never entirely rid himself of this fault, but in *My Southern Home*, his last book, he does have southern field Negroes talk and act like southern field Negroes.

The play *The Escape*, in five acts and seventeen scenes, shows clearly that Brown knew nothing of the stage. Loosely constructed according to the formula of the day and marred by didacticism and heroic sentimentality, its chief characters are but pawns in the hands of Purpose. The heroine Melinda is the identical twin of Miralda; and Clotel might have been their mother. Except the pronounced black type, all Brown's women conform to the character pattern set by Charles Brockden Brown and the ancestral pattern established by Fenimore Cooper's Cora Munro. William Brown's women are all octoroons, quadroons, or, at the very least, mulattoes. The unconscious irony in creating such characters is very sharp, whispering his unmentionable doubt of the racial equality he preached. His characters are no more representative of the Negroes he was supposed to depict than are Eliza and Uncle Tom. His women are beautiful and charming, finely mannered, appealing. What did the women of the master class have that Melinda or Cynthia lacked?

"Poor Cynthia! I knew her well. She was a quadroon, and one of the most beautiful women I ever saw. She was a native of St. Louis, and had there an irreproachable character for virtue and propriety of conduct. Mr. Walker bought her for the New Orleans market, and took her down with him on one of the trips I made with him. Never shall I forget the circumstances of that voyage! On the first night that we were on board the steamboat, he directed me to put her in a stateroom that he had provided for her, apart from the other slaves. I had seen too much of the workings of slavery not to know what this meant. I accordingly watched him into the stateroom, and listened to hear what passed between them. I heard him make his base offers and her reject them. . . . Neither threats nor bribes prevailed, however, and he retired disappointed of his prey."[5]

Brown's work as historian and commentator is far more substantial than his work in the purely creative field. Two of his earlier historical works, *The Black Man* and *The Negro in the American Rebellion*, were but as notes for *The Rising Son*, a work comprehending not only the ancient history of the Negro race in Africa, but treating successively the great epochs in the racial career down to Brown's own day. Using key episodes and men as the basis for historical narratives of more than ordinary interest, *The Rising Son* is an outline of history rather than a detailed relation of it. In this work Brown's blunt prejudices are shown softened into calmer rationalism : the swords he usually ground are here beaten into crude ploughshares. It should not be expected that after fifty years he could change precipitantly and wholly, but there is no doubt that in the end the artistic core of him rose up to assert itself.

Even more evident of the victory of his artistic consciousness over his social consciousness is his last work, *My Southern*

*Home.* He came at last to the recognition of permanent literary values over the ephemeral sensational. He is a composed Brown in *My Southern Home*, writing charmingly and interestingly of experiences close to him and of people who are *people.* Humor and pathos, sense and nonsense are skillfully blended in pieces that show his narrative skill at its best. He does not avoid propaganda altogether, but he administers it sparingly and in sugar-coated doses. The warmth and sunshine of the South glows over his pages. It is completely right that *My Southern Home*, his last book, should be also his best.

Brown died in 1884 in Cambridge, Massachusetts, after a full life of devotion to the cause of freedom. His prose adds ballast to the whole mass of antislavery writing. His place in the social history of America and in the literary history of the American Negro is assured. The first Negro writer of the drama and the novel, he was also the first American man of color to earn his living by his pen. Undoubtedly Brown stands high in the impressive list of Americans of Negro blood.

§ 3

But both by the quality of their work and the superiority of their numbers the orators easily dominated those who worked for the cause of abolition. Until the World War no organization for the spreading of propaganda ever equaled the American Convention of Abolition Society. Scores of black men helped to lash up the antislavery passions of the Garrisonians and the Smithians. A great many men of mediocre talent were thrown into bold relief by the white-hot light of the passion of the times, and a great many others of fine gifts were thrown into utter shadow. No battle of tongues has been waged with so much personal hatred as that preceding the Civil War.

Among the great personalities who achieved eminent personal success during the period from 1835 to the turn of the century none was greater than Frederick Douglass. No man of his time achieved in so many fields through so many difficulties. No man of the time was better known than he, and only Lincoln was more honored (and more reviled) and better loved. His personality, so essential to the effectiveness of his work, flows through the times like a strong, calm tide.

Frederick Douglass was born a slave in Talbot County, Maryland, in or about 1817. For twenty-one years he remained in slavery, first on the plantation of Thomas Auld and later as a hired-out boat caulker in Baltimore, where he lived in the home of a relative of his master's. Here Douglass learned his first letters. Through the kindness of the mistress of the household he was taught to read along with the young son of the family, until the master of the house put a stop to it. Afterwards he was largely self-taught, ingeniously beguiling the young white boys of the neighborhood into telling him letters and words he did not know. When he came into possession of *The Columbian Orator*, a popular school book of the time, he felt that he had discovered a treasure. In his *Narrative* he tells us that the speeches of Sheridan, Lord Chatham, William Pitt, and Fox "were all choice documents." But even so, when he escaped to New York and settled in New Bedford, Massachusetts, in 1838 he was still far from literate. He learned to read more easily at the same time that he absorbed the abolitionist doctrine in the pages of the *Liberator*. "From this time I was brought into contact with the mind of Mr. Garrison, and his paper took a place in my heart second only to the Bible. . . . I loved this paper and its editor." It was not until he met Garrison in 1841, however, that Douglass definitely entered into the abolitionist movement.

His rise was rapid. By 1842 he had begun his first writing,

letters that were published in numerous antislavery journals. The chief characteristics of these early letters were their dignified scorn and calm and their humorless censure of the slavers and the slave institution. Many of them were auto-biographical. Later he was forced to use these open letters as instruments of defense against newspaper attacks that were made upon him. By 1845, when the first long autobiograph-ical account appeared, he had had to make at least four vigorous defenses of himself. That he did so with dignity is attested by the letters themselves, especially the one to Dr. Samuel Cox, one of the foremost churchmen of the day, who had stupidly attacked him.

The 1845 autobiography, *Narrative of the Life of Frederick Douglass*, came at a time when the writing of slave narra-tives, real or fictitious, was popular propaganda, but Doug-lass's book is in many ways too remarkable to be dismissed as mere hack writing. Contemporary criticism spoke in glowing and even extravagant terms of it. Modern criticism, though more conservative, is certainly warm. In utter con-trast to the tortured style of most of the slave biographies, Douglass's style is calm and modest. Even in this first book his sense of discrimination in the selection of details is fine and sure. The certainty of the book's emotional power is due in part to the stringent simplicity of style and in part to the ingenuous revelation of the author's character.

Because his freedom was endangered by the publication of the *Narrative*, in 1845 Douglass went abroad where he lectured in England, Scotland, and Ireland for two years. It was now that his letters to the press began to appear regularly not only in the antislavery organs, but in such exemplary papers as the *New York Tribune*, the *Brooklyn Eagle*, and the *London Post*. This experience in written de-bate sharpened his logic, and was to serve him importantly when he later established his own newspaper. Those months abroad were fruitful for Douglass, months of enlightenment. He made new and strong friends for himself and his cause. The same dignity with which his letters answered malicious attacks or set forth his arguments marked his speeches. Indeed, reading his letters now, one feels that they were written for speech, that Douglass made no difference between the written and the spoken word. Before his return to the States, the English Society of Friends had undertaken to raise seven hundred and fifty dollars for the purchase of his freedom.

That Douglass's outlook had broadened is reflected in his decision to discard the principle of disunion and to adopt the policy of freedom and union. His changed views meant the loss of friends and the closing of many channels, but he endured this without bitterness. It meant a break with Garrison, under whom a faction of abolitionists took the view that slavery should be destroyed by splitting the union. Douglass's view, stemming from England, held that the union should be preserved. Garrison's faction was strong. To give himself freer scope, Douglass moved to Rochester, New York, and established his own paper, *The North Star*, a weekly which was published as *Frederick Douglass' Paper* for thirteen years.

Except for work from the pen of Douglass, *The North Star* differed but little from other antislavery journals. Because of the force of Douglass's personality the paper won a high place in the field, but a great deal of the editor's energy was spent in securing funds to maintain publication. He mortgaged his home to that purpose. Strenuous programs of speechmaking engaged him, and many of his editorials were abstracts of his speeches. He grew greater as a speaker than as a writer. The speeches he made between 1849 and 1860 were never equaled in logic, in emotional force, or in simple clarity. His peculiarly stony denunciation, the calm bitterness of his irony, and his frequent use of the simple and emotional language of the Bible make the speeches of this period memorable examples of the oratorical art. His speech on American slavery, perhaps his greatest, delivered in celebration of Independence Day at Rochester, July 5, 1852, is an example :

"Why am I called upon to speak here today? What have I, or those I represent, to do with your national independence? Are the great principles of political freedom and of natural justice embodied in that Declaration of Independence extended to us? And am I, therefore, called upon to bring our humble offering to the national altar, and to confess the benefits, and express devout gratitude for the blessings resulting from your independence to us? . . . What, to the American slave, is your Fourth of July? I answer ; a day that reveals to him more than all other days in the year, the gross injustice and cruelty to which he is a constant victim."

He says further, quoting the 137th Psalm :

"We hanged our harps upon the willows in the midst thereof. For there they that carried us away captive required of us a song ; and they that wasted us required of us mirth, saying, Sing us one of the songs of Zion. How shall we sing the Lord's song in a strange land? If I forget thee, O Jerusalem, let my right hand forget her cunning. If I do not remember thee, let my tongue cleave to the roof of my mouth."[6]

When *The North Star* became an organ of Gerrit Smith's Liberty party and was thereafter called *Frederick Douglass' Paper*, Douglass was still burdened with financing it. His entrance into politics was the one further step which he saw as a means of helping his people. By the late 1850's he had come to the conclusion that the abolition of slavery was not enough ; that, when abolition did come, the Negro must have the right to vote in order to be completely free. "Liberty is meaningless where the right to utter one's thoughts and opinions has ceased to exist; and what more tangible evidence of that right can be found than in the ballot?" From this time on his expressions from the platform and in the press are more and more burdened with this thought.

In 1855 the autobiographical *My Bondage and My Freedom* was published. His style, still without tricks, proves surer. Considerably longer than his first book, its length is amply justified by its matter. Though the first part follows in general the simple plan of the *Narrative*, he acquaints us more intimately with slavery and expresses his more mature thoughts on the problems which he faced. It is evident, especially when he writes of his English trip, that his knowledge of men had grown. Equally evident in the logic and sincerity of his arguments is the growth of his knowledge of issues. Garrison's charges are here fully answered. *My Bondage and My Freedom* is the high mark of the second stage of Douglass's career. Indeed, though for many years after 1865 he was active as both speaker and writer, and though his thoughts steadily matured, he did not exceed the emotional pitch of this second period. As his intellectual vigor increased (and became, it may be said, a little warped by the over-development of his capacity for irony), his emotional and artistic powers fell off. By the 1880's he was not an orator speaking with a spontaneous overflow of emotion: he was a finished public speaker, more concerned with intellectual than emotional responses.

Douglass's aroused powers of thought made it possible for him to do a work that grew steadily in importance. Emotionally drunk, men had become intellectually blind to the true status of the Negro. A great many people seemed to think that abolition was a calm bay through which the black race would sail to some safe harbor. Few saw that harbors had yet to be constructed. It was this task that Douglass now engaged in. He accepted abolition as a future certainty and looked far beyond it. The material of his speeches, many of which were printed as pamphlets, shows the new tack he had taken. In 1854 he spoke on the Negro from the ethnological point of view. The next year in his paper and on the platform he sought to interpret the Constitution, climaxing his efforts with a reasonable argument that the Constitution is antislavery in a pamphlet entitled *The Constitution of the United States: Is it Pro-Slavery or Anti-Slavery?* Late in the fifties his pamphlet dealing with the epochal Dred Scott Decision was published. Douglass continued this line when he fled to England in 1860 after President James Buchanan sent agents to arrest him for the part he was supposed to have played in John Brown's uprising. And after the Civil War (during which he had helped to organize the Fifty-fourth and Fifty-fifth Massachusetts Negro regiments under Colonel Shaw), he argued that complete enfranchisement of the Negro was the logical end of freedom.

After the presidential campaign that resulted in Lincoln's election, Douglass threw himself more and more into politics. He was a prominent figure in the Philadelphia assemblage of the National Loyalists' Convention in 1866, having been elected to represent the city of Rochester. Resolutions passed at that convention after Douglass's speech in favor of Negro enfranchisement had their bearing upon the subsequent passage of the Fifteenth Amendment.

From this point in his career onward, Douglass became not only the intellectual leader of the Negro, but the political leader as well. He remained active as a speaker, but a great many of the speeches of this period were run-of-the-mine political speeches and commemorative orations. His work as editor of the *New National Era* from 1869 to 1873 and the work on his third book, *Life and Times of Frederick Douglass*, absorbed his best energies. *Life and Times* was published in 1881. Its interest comes authentically from the man's life and thought. It has been called properly the most American of American life stories. Unconsciously, with no fanfare of self-satisfaction, the story develops the dramatic theme from bondage to the council tables of a great nation. It is written with the same lucid simplicity that marks all of Douglass's best work, but there is still the lack of differentiation between speaker and writer. *Life and Times* is his best book.

It remained for him to do yet one other book. Between 1880 and the year of his death his political activities brought personal rewards, which he used to benefit his people. Three presidents—Grant, Garfield, and Harrison—appointed him United States Marshal, Recorder of Deeds, and Minister to Haiti respectively. In 1886 he visited England, Ireland, and Scotland for the third time. He took part in celebrations, demonstrations and protests, and was in the van of movements calculated to improve the position of American Negroes. All of these experiences went into a larger edition of *Life and Times*, which was issued in 1892.

This final work is slow and repetitious. His powers had waned, but he was still aware that all was not finished. He had mellowed with only slight decay ; grown into acceptance without resignation. To the last, he wrote as he spoke.

"I have seen dark hours in my life, and I have seen the darkness gradually disappearing, and the light gradually increasing. One by one I have seen obstacles removed, errors corrected, prejudices softened, proscriptions relinquished, and my people advancing in all the elements that make up the sum of general welfare. I remember that God reigns in eternity, and that, whatever delays, disappointments, and discouragements may come, truth, justice, liberty, and humanity will prevail."

The literary work of Douglass is first important as examples of a type and period of American literature. Many of his speeches rank with the best of all times and are included in collections of the finest oratorical art. That at least two of his books, *My Bondage and My Freedom* and the first *Life and Times*, have not been recognized for what they are is attributable more to neglect than to the judgment of honest inquiry. Certainly no American biographies rank above them in the literary qualities of simplicity, interest, and compression of style. They delineate from an exceptional point of view a period in the history of the United States than which no other is more fraught with drama and sociological significance. By any standard his work ranks high.

That he was easily the most important figure in American Negro literature at the time of his death goes without saying. He was the very core of the For Freedom group, fitting his art more nearly to his purposes than any of the others— and suffering less intrinsically for doing it. Without him the For Freedom group would be destitute of true greatness, Negro literature would be poorer, and American literary fields of oratory and autobiography would be lacking a figure in whom they might justly claim pride.

Douglass died in February, 1895, at Anacostia, D. C. His home there has been converted into a shrine, and the citizens of Rochester, New York, for twenty-five years his place of residence, have erected a public monument to him.

§ 4

In 1854, while Douglass was climbing in importance as the spokesman and ideal of the Negro race, there appeared in Philadelphia a thin volume called *Poems on Miscellaneous Subjects*, by Frances Ellen Watkins. The title is significant, for it indicates a different trend in the creative urge of the Negro. Except for Jupiter Hammon and Phillis Wheatley, Negro writers up to this time were interested mainly in the one theme of slavery and in the one purpose of bringing about freedom. The treatment of their material was doctrinal, definitely conditioned to the ends of propaganda. A willful (and perhaps necessary) monopticism had blinded them to other treatment and to the possibilities in other subjects. It remained for Miss Watkins, with the implications in the title of her volume, to attempt a redirection.

The writers did not immediately follow the lead. William Wells Brown, for an instance, only partly rejected doctrinal treatment in his later work. It was not until the late sixties, following the war, that Douglass's speeches rang changes on his material. Novels, short stories, and essays, though milder than the dozens of slave biographies, autobiographies, and "accounts" published earlier, were still infected by the deadly virus when Charles Chesnutt began his literary career at the turn of the century. But attempts had been made to bring about a truer artistic outlook.

In 1861 Mrs. Harper (Frances Ellen Watkins) wrote to Thomas Hamilton, the editor of the *Anglo-African*, a monthly journal that had been established the year before: "If our talents are to be recognized we must write less of issues that are particular and more of feelings that are general. We are blessed with hearts and brains that compass more than ourselves in our present plight. . . . We must look to the future which, God willing, will be better than the present or the past, and delve into the heart of the world."[7]

It seems that Hamilton was influenced by this admonition. He did his best to make his magazine a broad cultural organ for black American expression, a Negro-manned duplicate of the *North American Review* or the *Atlantic Monthly*. In the very nature of things at that time he could not succeed, but one meets in the pages of the *Anglo-African* articles and essays on the theater, on agronomy, on literature, and on the colonization movement, sermons on many subjects, and a few stories without the predominant bias. Now and then the work of this kind hit the farthest extreme, as in most of the work of Phillis Wheatley.

To what degree Frances Ellen Watkins followed her own advice can be judged from her writings. In one sense she was a trail blazer, hacking, however ineffectually, at the dense forest of propaganda and striving to "write less of issues that were particular and more of feelings that were general." But she was seriously limited by the nature and method of her appeal. Immensely popular as a reader ("elocutionist"), the demands of her audience for the sentimental treatment of the old subjects sometimes overwhelmed her. On the occasions when she was free "to delve into the heart of the world" she was apt to gush with pathetic sentimentality over such subjects as wronged innocence, the evils of strong drink, and the blessed state of childhood.

*Poems on Miscellaneous Subjects* was published when Miss Watkins was twenty-nine years old. It is evident from the poems in this volume that she had not thought out the artistic creed later indited to Thomas Hamilton. Her topics are slavery and religion, and these first poems mark her as a full-fledged member of the propagandist group. The volume sold ten thousand copies within five years and was reprinted three times before her next work, *Moses, A Story of the Nile*, appeared in 1869. *Sketches of Southern Life* came in 1873 and her fourth volume, published without date, was called *The Sparrows Fall and Other Poems*.[8]

At first she was sometimes tense and stormy, as in "Bury Me In a Free Land":

> I ask no monument, proud and high,
> To arrest the gaze of the passer-by;
> All that my yearning spirit craves
> Is bury me not in a land of slaves.[9]

After *Moses* Miss Watkins tended more frequently to the maudlin. Her later volumes show her of larger compass but of less strength than does the first. Though she held conventional views on most of the social evils of the day, at her best she attacked them in a straightforward manner. A few lines from "The Double Standard" show her method:

> Crime has no sex and yet today
>     I wear the brand of shame;
> Whilst he amid the gay and proud
>     Still bears an honest name.
>
> .    .    .    .    .
>
> Yes blame me for my downward course,
>     But Oh! remember well,
> Within your homes you press the hand
>     That led me down to hell.
>
> .    .    .    .    .
>
> No golden weights can turn the scale
>     Of justice in His sight;
> And what is wrong in woman's life
>     In man's cannot be right.[10]

Miss Watkins wrote a great many sentimental ballads in obvious imitation of the ballads which appeared with monotonous regularity in *Godey's Lady's Book* and other popular monthlies. The ballad form was well suited to some of her material and was an excellent elocutionary pattern. Even now the recitation of the piece "The Dying Bondman" has not lost its effectiveness.

> By his bedside stood the master
> Gazing on the dying one,

Knowing by the dull gray shadows
That life's sands were almost run.

"Master," said the dying bondman,
"Home and friends I soon shall see;
But before I reach my country,
Master write that I am free;

Give to me the precious token,
That my kindred dead may see—
Master! write it, write it quickly!
Master write that I am free!"

.    .    .    .    .

Eagerly he grasped the writing;
"I am free!" at last he said.
Backward fell upon the pillow.
He was free among the dead.[11]

Practically all the social evils from the double standard of sex morality to corruption in politics were lashed with the scourge of her resentment. Her treatment of these topics never varied: she traced the effects of the evil upon some innocent—a young and dying girl, as in "A Little Child Shall Lead Them," or a virtuous woman, as in "The Double Standard," or a sainted mother, as in "Nothing and Something." But her treating these evils at all entitles her to respect and gratitude as one who created other aims and provided new channels for the creative energies of Negro writers.

In some of Miss Watkins's verse one thing more is to be noted especially. In the volume called *Sketches of Southern Life* the language she puts in the mouths of Negro characters has a fine racy, colloquial tang. In these poems she managed to hurdle a barrier by which Dunbar was later to feel himself tripped. The language is not dialect. She retained the speech patterns of Negro dialect, thereby giving herself greater emotional scope (had she wished or had the power to use it) than the humorous and the pathetic to which it is generally acknowledged dialect limits one. In all of her verse Miss Watkins attempted to suit her language to her theme. In *Moses* she gives her language a certain solemnity and elevation of tone. In her pieces on slavery she employs short, teethy, angry monosyllables. Her use of dialectal patterns was no accident. She anticipated James Weldon Johnson.

Miss Watkins's prose is less commendable than her poetry, though here, too, she made a departure by trying the short story form. Her prose is frankly propagandic. The novel *Iola Leroy; or, Shadows Uplifted*, published in 1893, was written in "the hope to awaken in the hearts of our countrymen a stronger sense of justice and a more Christlike humanity in behalf of those whom the fortunes of war threw homeless, ignorant, and poor, upon the threshold of a new era." It is a poor thing as a novel, or even as a piece of prose, too obviously forced and overwritten, and too sensational to lift it from the plane of the possible to the probable. Her short stories, two of which were published in the *Anglo-African*, were no better in kind. Her knowledge of slave life and of slave character was obviously secondhand, and the judgments she utters on life and character are conventional and trite. As a writer of prose Miss Watkins is to be remembered rather for what she attempted than for what she accomplished.

In general Miss Watkins was less confined than any of her contemporaries. Her poetry can be grouped under four heads—religious poems, traditional lyrics of love and death, antislavery poems, and poems of social reform, of which the antislavery group is not the largest. Her poetry was not unduly warped by hatred. Like Horton, whom she probably knew in his later years, she gave to some of her pieces a lightness of touch that was sadly lacking in most of the heavy-footed writing of her race. A great deal of her poetry was written to be recited, and this led her into errors of metrical construction which, missed when the poems are spoken, show up painfully on the printed page. In all but her long, religious narrative, *Moses,* simplicity of thought and expression is the keynote.

She was the first Negro woman poet to stand boldly forth and glory in her pride of race, but she was not too vindicative. Her ambition to be the pivot upon which Negro writers were to turn to other aims, to compass more than themselves in their racial plight, was not accomplished. But before her death in 1911, the movement of which she had been the first champion had a brief and brilliant revival.

§ 5

The work of James Madison Bell brings this chapter to a fitting close, for he wrote less to accomplish freedom than in praise of it after it had been won. He gave freedom and the heroes who had fought for it the poetic salvos he thought so richly appropriate, swelling the final great chorus of crude music that roared out through the dark times of preparation and through the din of the years of war.

Bell was a rover—a sort of vagabond poet, lecturer, and plasterer—living at various times in Gallipolis and Cincinnati, Lansing and Detroit, and Canada. In this latter place he became friend and counselor to the insurrectionist John Brown, and only "escaped the fate of many of John Brown's men by the Providence of God." On his wanderings, combining the practical and the ideal, he followed his trade of master plasterer, recited his poetry in public gatherings, and "proclaimed the truth and doctrines of human liberty, instructed and encouraged his race to noble deeds and to great activity in building up their new homes." With a full and active life, the "Bard of the Maumee," or the "Poet of Hope" (both of which titles he unblushingly claimed) brings to a close a full and active period.

Most of Bell's verse is of the inspirational kind. He seemed to feel it his especial duty to encourage his people through commemorating events and circumstances, men and opinions that seemed to him noble. His pages thunder with lofty references to Lincoln, Douglass, Day, Garrison, John Brown, and others. Most of his poems suffer from being too long, many of them running to more than two hundred lines and two to more than a thousand. That he had neither the skill nor the power to sustain pieces of such length is evidenced by the steady drop in emotional force and the frequent shifting of metrical form within a poem.

Bell's *Poetical Works* is unusual and therefore interesting. He had read a good many of the "popular immortals" and one can see their influence at work on him. He attempted imitations of Pope and Scott, Tennyson and Bryant. His long, expository narratives are veritable melting pots of styles and treatments :

> This is proud Freedom's day!
> Swell, swell the gladsome day,
>   Till earth and sea
> Shall echo with the strain
> Through Britain's vast domain ;
> No bondman clanks his chain,
>   All men are free.
>
> Of every clime, of every hue,
>   Of every tongue, of every race,
> 'Neath heaven's broad ethereal blue ;

Oh! let thy radiant smiles embrace,
Till neither slave nor one oppressed
   Remain throughout creation's span,
By thee unpitied and unblest,
   Of all the progeny of man.[12]

What Bell attempted in most of his longer pieces is illustrated by the introductory "arguments" of two of them :

"The Progress of Liberty is delineated in the events of the past four years—the overthrow of the rebellion, the crushing of the spirit of anarchy, the total extinction of slavery, and the return of peace and joy to our beloved country.

"The invincibility of Liberty is illustrated in the beautiful episode of the Swiss patriot, William Tell, wherein the goddess is personified by an eagle towering amidst the clouds.

"The poet claims the full enfranchisement of his race from political, as well as personal thraldom, and declares that the progress of Liberty will not be complete until the ballot is given the loyal freedman.

"The noble actions and self-sacrificing spirit of the immortal Lincoln is next sung, and in mournful strains the poet bewails his martyrdom. This concludes with a touching eulogy on our sainted martyr.

"The reconstruction policy of President Johnson is reviewed, and, while objecting, he does not wholly condemn his motives, but warns the ruling powers that unless the spirit of rebellion is wholly obliterated and every vestige swept away, it will only slumber to awake again with renewed ferocity."[13]

"The poet laments the discord of his harp, and its disuse, until answering Freedom's call he again essays its harmony. He portrays the conflict and gives thanks to God for the dawning day of Freedom. He rejoices that Columbia is free ; he eulogizes the moral heroes, and describes how America is 'Marching on' in the footsteps of the war-like 'Hero John'."[14]

It is not known when Bell died, but he lived and died not without honor. In a biographical sketch of him Bishop B. W. Arnett of the A. M. E. Church praised him unstintingly, especially as the poet of liberty. Before Bell's impetuous full song the last of the Negro's bitterness against slavery was swept away, but the "sweetness of the liberty" of which he sang seemed turned to wormwood on the tongues of his successors. Had he lived beyond the first decade of the twentieth century, he perhaps would have been less sure of the uninterrupted progress of Liberty than when he wrote:

> Ride onward, in thy chariot ride,
> Thou peerless queen; ride on, ride on—
> With Truth and Justice by thy side!
> From pole to pole, from sun to sun![15]

§ 6

After Jupiter Hammon and Phillis Wheatley, the work of the writers of the period covering the more than one hundred years from 1770 to 1890 shows their devotion to one increasing purpose. They lived precariously through a trying period of the most significant action. Most of them were far too much engaged with the business of existence to devote hungry time to the more esthetic ends of art. Their work suffered enormously because of their personal subjection to the circumstances in which they lived. Strangely absent from their work is telling evidence of that gift of happy, spirit-saving laughter for which the race has been justly lauded. In place of this we find the acidulent disposition of Remond, the sharp and bitter irony of Douglass, and the blasts of Brown's impotent defenses. The writers and orators had not yet learned that "a laugh is the finest of foils." They felt compelled either to defend or prove—to defend themselves against the attacks of a largely inimicable society, or to prove that the Negro had important contributions to make and was as capable of intellectual and cultural achievement as the white man.

Excepting only Phillis Wheatley and Frederick Douglass, none of the writers of this period was an uncommon artist. Nearly all of them wrote to fulfill the requirements of elocution, knowing that certain metrical faults could be glossed over in recitation. They often sacrificed beauty of thought and of truth—the specific goals of art—to the exigencies of their particular purposes. But a great and good work was done. They created in the Negro a core of racial pride without which no great endeavor is possible. Though they were not artists enough to see and recognize with love and pride the beauty of their own unaffected spirituals, tales, and work songs, they nevertheless acknowledged the possibilities for artistic treatment in Negro peasant life, the southern scene, and the enigmatic soul of the simple Negro.

# 3. *Adjustment*

JAMES E. CAMPBELL, PAUL LAURENCE DUNBAR, CHARLES W. CHESNUTT, W. BURGHARDT DUBOIS, FENTON JOHNSON, WILLIAM S. BRAITHWAITE, AND OTHERS

§ I

The end of the Civil War brought about an overwhelming change in the position of the Negro in American life. This change was not confined to the liberation of the slaves. When both North and South had a little recovered from the stunning effects of the long months of hostilities, tension between Negroes and whites grew alarmingly. The failure of the President's reconstruction policy did not help matters. The gathered forces of intersectional bitterness were heaped upon the Negro. What had the war been about? What had been its purpose? To free the Negro. Was he not, then, responsible for the bloodshed, the pillage and ruin of the South? Thus reasoned the common minds in the South. Economically exploited by unscrupulous carpetbaggers and the land-rich on the one hand, the Negro was driven from pillar to post by the newly organized Vigilantes and the ignorant poor whites on the other. Federal intervention in many sections of the South, notably South Carolina, Tennessee, Mississippi, Florida, and Louisiana, restrained only temporarily the manner and the degree of exploitation. Crime rates—homicide, mayhem, and arson—leaped devilishly, not entirely because of the depredations of the newly freed Negro.

In the North conditions among Negroes were but little better. Industrial and race rioting broke out in numerous large cities. Negro churches and other places of assembly were fired. In some cities it was unsafe for days at a time for Negroes to walk the streets. No one knew how long it would be before a half-measure of adjustment was made.

The most they dared hope was for the South to settle into acceptance and acquiescence and the North soften into evasive and balm-like tolerance.

The Negro was quick to realize the profound danger in this state of affairs. But he had learned valuable lessons in slavery. He had learned to enter "with unconscious self-forgetfulness into the purposes, plans, and aspirations of other people."[1] He had acquired a knowledge and command of the white man's psychology, and he molded and tempered his actions and attitudes in the light of this knowledge. If the Negro knew anything, he knew that laughter was his instrument now as it had been under the lash, the broiling sun, and the threats of being sold down the river. He pursued the gods of servile laughter as another race might pursue the god of war. He sang his gay nonsense music, the laughing, desperate music of heartbreak. He made jokes and turned them upon himself. He became a minstrel, a buffoon.

The minstrel tradition was not altogether new. It had its origin among slaves about the year 1820. "Every plantation had its talented band that could crack jokes, and sing and dance to the accompaniment of banjo and bones. . . . There is a record of at least one of these bands that became semi-professional and travelled from plantation to plantation giving performances."[2] The step from semiprofessionalism in the days of slavery to professionalism after the emancipation was a short and, in the nature of things, a necessary one. Certainly it cannot be denied that the fun-provoking genius of the Negro was put to good use. Through it he won gradually a good-natured, condescending tolerance. Because of it he came to be treated with the mock despair of a master for a lazy, shiftless servant who eats, sleeps, but does no work, and of whom he cannot be rid. He was congratulated on his powers of mimicry and his unimportant, but interesting gift of song : and he was being paid for them. It sounds little now, but in that day it was much.

But something less propitious was happening too. By a sort of natural development the "darky" sketches, now so intimately a part of American minstrelsy, hardened into the recognized speech of the Negro, into glee and jamboree songs that were immediately characterized as "coon" songs, into sentimental ballads which were considered especially representative of the colored people, and finally into a pathetic kind of "darky" poetry. Thus were set up the limits to the Negro's media of expression. Thus was focused the picture of the Negro as a slapstick and a pathetic buffoon.

It was not long before the Negro's willful impositions began to make heartbreaking demands upon him. It was not long before he discovered that in order to be heard at all he must speak in the voice and accents that his hearers recognized. The picture of Paul Dunbar as a thwarted poet yearning to escape the conventions of dialect, which James Weldon Johnson draws in *Black Manhattan*, is fairly composite. Subsequent to Dunbar (he died in 1906) and, indeed, even as late as the second decade of the present century, serious literary men of color found it hard to go beyond the limits of popular concept and to destroy the picture of themselves as it had been purposefully created in the mind of white America.

§ 2

Two men of serious artistic inclinations preceded Dunbar in the use of dialect as a medium for poetic expression. James Edwin Campbell, the first of these, owes his importance in this study entirely to the fact that he was the first Negro poet to use dialect consistently. Campbell's dialect is more nearly a reproduction of plantation Negro speech sounds than that of any other writer in American literature.

Joel Chandler Harris's dialect is skillful and effective misrepresentation, a made language in every sense of the word, conveying the general type impression of untaught imagination, ignorance, and low cunning with which he believed the Negro endowed. Paul Dunbar's dialect is a bastard form, modeled closer upon James Whitcomb Riley's colloquial language than upon the speech it was supposed to represent. Campbell's ear alone dictated his language. Dunbar's five senses (as they should) controlled his. The wide difference is shown nowhere more effectively than in a stanza from a poem by each. Campbell's "My Merlindy Brown" :

> O, de light-bugs glimmer down de lane,
>   Merlindy! Merlindy!
> O, de whip-will callin' notes ur pain—
>   Merlindy, O, Merlindy!
> O, honey lub, my turkle dub,
>   Doan you hyah my bawnjer ringin',
> While de night-dew falls an' de bo'n owl calls
> By de ol bo'n gate Ise singin'.[3]

Dunbar's "When Malindy Sings" :

> Fiddlin' man jes' stop his fiddlin'
>   Lay his fiddle on de she'f :
> Mockin'bird quit try'n to whistle
>   'Cause he jes' so shamed hisse'f.
> Folks a-playin' on de banjo
>   Draps dey fingahs on de strings—
> Bless yo' soul—fergits to move 'em,
>   When Malindy sings.[4]

Campbell tried to write poems in the pure English also, but he was not successful. His best work is done in the Negro

dialect lyrics, some of which have been set to music by Harry
T. Burleigh. The type of work Campbell did may be taken
as fairly representative of the work that was being done by
dozens of now forgotten white and Negro writers from the
late eighties onward. The conventions as to language and
racial character-concept were well established by the time
Campbell wrote. They had been sung and stammered, pan-
tomined and danced home by the minstrels. Campbell
translated them into rhyme. It remained now only to conform.

The other man who preceded Dunbar was in the perfect
minstrel tradition. In his work in dialect the tendency comes
to its ripest (one is tempted to write "rottenest") fruitage.

Daniel Webster Davis was born in North Carolina in 1862
and was educated in the colored schools of Richmond, Virginia, where he later taught. Finally taking up the ministry
as a profession, Davis turned his pulpit into a stage and soon
gained wide popularity as a reader and writer of dialect
pieces. He was a showman, but there is in his buffoonery a
peculiar sincerity, an apparent conviction that the way for
the Negro was the way of cheerful, prideless humility, and
that his ultimate lot was dependency. The implications of
the satiric shafts he directed against his race are inescapable.
He wrote for a white audience in a way which he knew would
please them.

> My Sarah Ann don' b'leve in signs,
>   Sense she don' bin to skule;
> She say we folks ain't got no sense,
>   An' almos' calls us fools.
> Wid all de changes she don' made,
>   One thing I know fur sho',
> She don' bresh all de cobwebs down,
>   But de horseshoe's ober de do'.

An 'tother day she start to church
   Wid all her fal-de-rals,
'Long Lucy Ann an' 'Rushy Jeems,
   An' lots er yuther gals ;
But when she had to turn erroun'
   Fur sumpin' she fergits,
She meks a cross-mark on de groun'
   An' turns erroun' an' spits.

.     .     .     .     .

So 'tiz wid ebry cullud chil',
   Do' it may be my own,
De skules kin nebber 'raderkate
   De thing dats in de bon'—
While folks is gittin' smart, ez sho'
   Ez whitewash made frum lime,
I gwine b'leve what de Bible sez
   Eerbout signs ub de times.[5]

So much of the poetry in the volume *'Weh Down Souf and Other Poems* (his only book) is in this same vein that it is not hard to believe the author's sincerity. On no more evidence than the character of the pieces in *'Weh Down Souf* it is not too much to attribute to him the anonymous "Common Sense," a broadside that appeared probably about 1897, the time of his book.

The time am ripe to take account
   Of whut we'se gwine t'do—
Is we a-aimin' to bus' out
   An' git us shot clean thu?
Or is we a'ter peaceful ways
   Eroun' de cabin do',
To 'joy de white man's blessin'
   Fur now an' ebermo'?[6]

Even in the odd and infrequent pieces in pure English in which he seems to express a somewhat different attitude, he is not very stimulating. These pieces, with their Pollyanna reasoning and their justification of the ways of God to black men, remind one of Phillis Wheatley.

E'en in our slavery we can trace the kindly
    hand of God,
That took us from our sunny land and from our
    native sod,
Where, clad in nature's simplest garb, man
    roamed a savage wild,
Untamed his passions; half a man and half a
    savage child,

But God, to teach him His dear will, saw fit
    to bring him where
He learned of Him and Jesus Christ those lessons
    rich and rare.
He made the savage into man, tho' moulded by
    the rod;
And Ethiopia has, indeed, stretched forth her
    hands to God.[7]

Much more wholesome are his rollicking folk versions of Bible stories, the kind of thing for which John Jasper, Black Billy Sunday, Brother Easter, and other Negro preachers of the day were so well known.

I know y'all long bin won'drin' how de chil-
    lun crossed de sea;
'Tiz jes' ez plain ez kin be to er 'sper'enced
    man like me.
You see, 'twuz in de winter when de chilluns
    dar wuz led,

An' de norf win' wuz a-blowin' strong ernuff
    to raise de dead.
Now, yo' see, de thing wuz easy, an' likewise
    berry nice,
Fur all de chillun had to do wuz to skeet across
    on ice.[8]

This is minstrel verse at its highest pitch of effectiveness.
The work of this kind represents the highest imaginative
power of the plantation Negro, the prodigal richness of his
imagery, and his happy power to resolve all difficulties and
mysteries with the reasoning of a child. Davis's contribution
to this type of expression is not inconsiderable.

§ 3

How tenacious, demanding, and circumscribing the dialect tradition and its concomitants had become before the
turn of the century is illustrated in the poet Paul Laurence
Dunbar. No Negro of finer artistic spirit has been born in
America, and none whose fierce, secret energies were more
powerfully directed toward breaking down the vast wall of
emotional and intellectual misunderstanding within which
he, as poet, was immured.

Dunbar was born to former slaves in Dayton, Ohio, in
June, 1872. Well known are the stories of his struggle to get
through high school, where he was made editor of the school
paper and class poet, and of his years as the "elevator poet"
until 1893, when his first volume, *Oak and Ivy*, was privately
printed. Not so well known is the fact that his most serious
efforts in *Oak and Ivy* and *Majors and Minors*, his second book,
are given to the pieces in pure English. Scarcely known at
all is the fact that all of his life he fervently sought to win
recognition as a master of the pure tongue. His own lines
express his disappointment:

But ah, the world, it turned to praise
A jingle in a broken tongue.[9]

The strength of the minstrel tradition can be blamed for
the comparative neglect of Dunbar's work in the pure medium. In language that is kind (but unconsciously deceptive),
William Dean Howells, Dunbar's first important literary
champion, voiced the prevailing attitude:

"Yet it appeared to me then, and it appears to me now,
that there is a precious difference of temperament between
the races which it would be a great pity ever to lose, and that
this is best preserved and most charmingly suggested by Mr.
Dunbar in those pieces of his where he studies the moods
and traits of his own race in its own accents of our English.
We call these pieces dialect pieces for want of some closer
phrase, but they are really not dialect so much as delightful
personal attempts and failures for the written and spoken
language. In nothing is his essentially refined and delicate
art so well shown as in these pieces, which, as I ventured to
say, described the range between appetite and emotion,
with certain lifts far beyond and above it, which is the range
of the race. He reveals in these a finely ironical perception
of the Negro's limitations, with a tenderness for them which
I think so very rare as to be almost quite new. I should say,
perhaps, that it was this humorous quality which Mr. Dunbar had added to our literature, and it would be this which
would most distinguish him, now and hereafter. It is something that one feels in nearly all the dialect pieces; and I
hope that in the present collection he has kept all of these
in his earlier volume, and added others to them."[10]

No wonder is it that toward the end of his hard, brief
career Dunbar is reported to have said that his best literary
friends had been also his worst enemies.

If we include his novels and short stories, far more than

half of Dunbar's writing is not in dialect at all. He realized
the limitations of the broken tongue. In those years of his
courtship and marriage, he could not use it to express his
rapturous love and joy. In the time of the slow decay of his
body and the wilting of his spirit, he found it inadequate
to his sick despair. "Paul himself," his wife once said of him,
"never spoke in dialect." It is easy to see what she meant.
The relation of medium to matter is relative, but of medium
to spirit absolute. When he wrote dialect he used himself
merely as the sympathetic expressive instrument of the
thoughts and feelings of others. When he wrote purely, he
wrote himself.

If there are times when his English pieces achieved only
a sentimental pathos, there are other times when he wrought
lyrics of delicate beauty. Primarily a lyrist, the music of
words is one of his chief charms. The so-called semiclassical
composers have realized this, and now some of Dunbar's
lyrics are better known on the programs of concert soloists
than in the pages of his books.

> Thou art the soul of a summer's day,
> Thou art the breath of the rose.
>> But the summer is fled
>> And the rose is dead
> Where are they gone, who knows,
>> who knows?

> Thou art the blood of my heart o' hearts,
> Thou art my soul's repose,
>> But my heart grows numb
>> And my soul is dumb.
> Where art thou, love, who knows,
>> who knows?

Thou art the hope of my after years—
Sun of my winter snows,
But the years go by
'Neath a clouded sky.
Where shall we meet, who knows,
who knows?[11]

Not only did Dunbar use pure English for more than half his poetry, he used it for all his novels and most of his short stories. Perhaps this was a mistake. It may have been that he could have done as fine a work in the dialect short tale as Charles Chesnutt was to do. "The Case of 'Ca'line,'" a story in the folk tradition, helps support this view. Excepting only a few of his short stories, Dunbar invariably falls short in prose fiction. His failure is twofold : he did not understand fully the extreme adaptability of folk material; and he did not study the art of prose fiction. The result of the first is that nearly all the folk stories are limited to burlesque, while the result of the second is that some very fine story stuff is hopelessly bungled.

It is, however, in his prose that Dunbar more nearly expressed the Negro, though rather as champion than as an artistically objective creator.

It is not strange to find Dunbar emerging as the spokesman of his race. The racial psychology says that though a man is kept down because of his color, he rises by virtue of it. Race pressure, the unuttered challenge flung at him by thousands of his people, would have made it necessary even if his own temperament had been disinclined to it. Excepting now (and only quite recently) the Russian and the German, no group imposes upon its artists demands as great as does the Negro.

But champions are notably more effective in poetry than

in prose. Poetry has the strength of conciseness : it can be made amusing and bitter, satirical and dramatic all in a few lines. It allows for anything, so it be poetry. But when propaganda enters into prose fiction it acquires necessarily some of the broad solidity of the prosaic medium, and this firm quality immediately puts the reader on the defensive. The reader's reaction is as of one being gulled, being shown a thing for the good of his soul. These are the things one comes to feel in too many of the stories of Dunbar. Like a leaden ghost, Purpose treads the print of "Silas Jackson," "The Ingrate," "One Man's Fortunes," and "Shaft 11." Not only is the technique of the stories faulty, but plausible, char- acter-derived motivation and convincing situation are lack- ing. The story that brushes aside esthetic ends must be fault- less in construction and style in order to succeed. It must captivate by sheer perfection of form. Dunbar was not aware of this. He brought to this difficult art only a zest in the message of his serious tales, and an instinctive sense of the humor inherent in certain situations in his burlesque stories. The latter are saved from failure ; but a story representative of the former, "The Strength of Gideon," with its powerful theme and well-defined plot, boils off in the end to a watery pottage.

The gem of Dunbar's stories is "The Trustfulness of Polly." In it Dunbar did not seek to express the Negro, but to re- create him. It was written in 1899, five years before his writing career ended, but he never again found such per- fect focus of characterization, motivation, theme, plot, and style. It is a story of the low-life school, a type that was not to become popular until twenty years after Dunbar's death. It deals with that insidious evil (then as now) in the life of the New York Negro, the policy game. "The Trustfulness of Polly" is the first story of Negro low-life in New York written by a Negro. Not only is it significant as the forerunner of the long list of low-life stories from *Home to Harlem* to *Beale Street*, but it presaged the courageous, if misled, objectivity with which the post-war Negro artist was to see the life of his people.

With the exception of *The Sport of the Gods*, Dunbar's novels are as different in tone, treatment, and ideas from his short stories as it is possible for them to be. In them he carried his rebellion against the minstrel tradition to the extreme of repudiating race. But he came face to face with bitter irony. He saw clearly that even his own life story— the unfolding of his youthful spiritual struggles, his yearnings and ambitions—would not seem true to a people who knew the Negro only as a buffoon. There had been Negroes generally known to America as anything but buffoons, but they were oddities, "exceptional because of their white blood." The story of a Negro boy living through Dunbar's experiences would not win credence. Negroes simply could not have certain emotional and spiritual things happen to them. So, in the novel *The Uncalled*, Dunbar, for the sake of plausibility (so little does realism have to do with truth), characterized himself as Frederick Brent, a white youth.

In two other novels, *The Love of Landry* and *The Fanatics*, he went even further. He drew white characters in typical white environment and sought to inspire the whole with the breath of living truth. He worked on an assumption which the minstrel tradition had consistently denied. He took forcibly the stand that Dumas and Pushkin, products of entirely different milieus, had come into naturally. Fundamentally, he said, there is no difference between Negro and white : the artist is free to work in whatever material he wishes. This was more than letting an imaginary white character stand for him ; this was standing for white characters. This was exchange—and of a most equalizing kind. He did not say that he was looking at white characters from a colored point of view. He simply assumed inherent emotional, intellectual, and spiritual identity with his characters. It had not been done before : except for a few scattered instances it has not been done in exactly this way since. Negro writers have assumed superiority over their low-life Negro characters. They have assumed for themselves, individually, equality with the white race, poking a desperately self-conscious fun at the minstrel Negro, in the manner of Irvin Cobb and Roy Cohen. They have assumed the white intellectual's point of view in dealing with Negroes as Carl Van Vechten deals with them. But they have not yet broached the fundamental assumption implicit in dealing with white characters in a white world. There are yet too many dicta against it.

That Dunbar's white novels are faulty proves only what is suggested by the faults of *The Sport of the Gods* : Dunbar was not a novelist. Because it deals with Negro characters, and because it was written after the discipline of the three other novels, *The Sport of the Gods* might be expected to be his best novel. But it is not. It is only his most interesting. As a blood and thunder tale of crime and retribution and as an analysis of the elements in the urban life of the Negro it does very well. As an artistic accomplishment it ranks below both *The Love of Landry* and *The Fanatics*.

But we must go back to Dunbar's verse, his dialect pieces, for though the necessity that drove him to dialect was bitter to him, he did his best work in this medium. His dialect pieces are not, however, most representative of his creative temper : they are merely what he had to do to win and hold his audience.

The comparison which is made so often between Paul Dunbar and Robert Burns, the Scottish poet, cannot fairly be taken further than to say that they were both singers. Burns's dialect was standard, a native tongue, understood by

all the Scots, representative of them and, therefore, broad
enough to give full expression to the people to whom it belonged. Burns's medium did not impose upon him the limitations to which the Negro poet was confined. On the other
hand, Dunbar's dialect was not native. It was not even representative of a few Negro communities. Had he imitated
the speech of the north Georgia Negro and uttered it among
the Geechees of south Georgia or the Gullahs of South Carolina he would not have been understood. Dunbar, from
scant knowledge of many dialects, made a language, a synthetic dialect that could be read with ease and pleasure by
the northern whites to whom dialect meant only an amusing
burlesque of Yankee English. Through such a bastard medium it was (and is) impossible to speak the whole heart of
a people. As James Weldon Johnson explains so thoroughly,[12]
dialect limited Dunbar to expressions of the humorous and
the pathetic.

> Ain't you kin' o' sad yo'se'f,
>     You little boots?
> Dis is all his mammy's lef',
>     Two little boots.
> Sence huh baby gone an' died
> Heav'n itse'f hit seem to hide
> Des a little bit inside
>     Two little boots.[13]

At verse of this kind Dunbar was a master. His sense of
rhythm and harmony, evident in whatever he wrote, makes
all the difference between his dialect pieces and the dialect
of dozens of his imitators. While he was sentimental, they
were vulgar and maudlin. While they bent at the knees with
coarse laughter, he was content with a gentle and pathetic
smile. While they blundered with dialect, he knew what

could be done with it and how far it could be made to go as a poetic medium. He knew the subjects it would fit—the sweet delight of calf love, the thrill of simple music, the querulousness of old age, the satisfactions of a full stomach, the distractions of an empty one, the time-mellowed pain of bereavement. He brought to these subjects a childlike quality, a hushed wonder that is the secret of his charm in them. At times, though, something sterner crept into the dialect pieces. He was not above touches of satire, cries of reproach, and even weary resignation to a life that at its best was extremely hard.

More often, however, he reserved the firmer tone for his pure English, going the way of challenging comparison in poetry that William Wells Brown had gone in prose, but doing it more effectively. Ignored by contemporary critics as this work was, it is principally by virtue of it that Dunbar holds the place of reverence in the hearts of Negroes. Negro school children, taught to scorn all dialect as a stamp of the buffoon, learn "Ode to Ethiopia," "Black Samson of Brandywine," "The Colored Soldiers," and several others. They have become one with the traditional learning of the race. "The Colored Soldiers" stirs the Negro in exactly the same way as "The Charge of the Light Brigade" stirred the Victorian Englishman.

> And at Pillow! God have mercy
>   On the deeds committed there,
> And the souls of those poor victims
>   Sent to Thee without a prayer.
> Let the fulness of Thy pity
>   O'er the hot wrought spirits sway
> Of the gallant colored soldiers
>   Who fell fighting on that day!

Yes, the Blacks enjoy their freedom,
    And they won it dearly, too;
For the life blood of their thousands
    Did the southern fields bedew.
In the darkness of their bondage,
    In the depths of slavery's night,
Their muskets flashed the dawning
    And they fought their way to light.

.    .    .    .    .

They have slept and marched and suffered
    'Neath the same dark skies as you,
They have met as fierce a foeman,
    And have been as brave and true.
And their deeds shall find a record
    In the registry of Fame;
For their blood has cleansed completely
    Every blot of Slavery's shame.
So all honor and all glory
    To those noble sons of Ham—
The gallant colored soldiers
    Who fought for Uncle Sam![14]

Such a poem as "The Colored Soldiers" marks him as being in one sense the spiritual father of James Weldon Johnson, Claude McKay, and a number of younger poets. But in these, as in his dialect pieces, Dunbar did not feel that he had fulfilled his larger self. He did not marvel, as does Cullen, that God had made a poet black and bade him sing. He was more concerned with singing than with blackness. He wanted to be known and remembered not as a black poet, but as a *poet*. The price he paid made his popularity among whites as dross to him. The tribute he paid

to his race was in kind no different from that paid by Tennyson as poet-laureate to his queen. Time and again he expresses his disappointment at "the world's disdain" of the
work which he himself held in the highest estimation.
The best of these pieces show a morbid concern with failure and death. He could not have been concerned with
failure as a dialect poet. His success in that line was assured.
It was the other failure he feared—and foresaw.

> Emblem of blasted hope and lost desire
>     No finger ever traced thy yellow page
>     Save Time's. Thou has not wrought to
>         noble rage
> The hearts thou wouldst have stirred. Not
>         any fire
> Save sad flames set to light a funeral pyre
>     Dost thou suggest. Nay,—impotent in age,
>     Unsought, thou holdest a corner of the
>         stage
> And ceasest even dumbly to aspire.
>
> How different was the thought of him that
>         writ.
>     What promised he to love of ease and
>         wealth,
>     When men should read and kindle at his wit.
> But here decay eats up the book by stealth,
> While it, like some old maiden solemnly,
> Hugs its incongruous virginity![15]

How right was Dunbar's judgment as to the worth of his
own poems is only partly our concern. It may be said, how-

ever, that if the poet is to be judged by his hold on the consciousness of his audience, Dunbar must rest content with the appeal of his dialect to his white audience and the grip of his eulogies on the hearts and minds of his Negro audience. Though certain of his pure English lines are frequently quoted, in general they are overlooked; not because they are poor, but because they do not distinguish him from dozens of other poets. And a poet, to succeed, must be distinguishable. Such poems as "Life," "We Wear the Mask," "Who Knows," and a half dozen others must be excluded from this general criticism.

As for the temper which fostered Dunbar's hopes, it is derived from Frances Ellen Watkins and consists in the awakening artistic consciousness, which in its perfect state permits of no racial limitations of matter and method. Through Dunbar and James Weldon Johnson this consciousness flows strong but less pure to the group of young writers who have been called "New Negroes." That the New Negroes have not attempted to do what Dunbar did in prose is perhaps a mark of their wisdom. But their spirit is much the same. Many years must elapse before white America (the audience for whom books are published and to whom books are sold) will accept white American novels by Negroes. Poetry has moved less slowly, and certain Negro poets stand today as proof that Dunbar's spirit was right. As regards his white audience in general, Dunbar's words in, "The Poet," will probably remain true:

> He sang of love when earth was young,
> And Love, itself was in his lays.
> But ah, the world, it turned to praise
> A jingle in a broken tongue.[16]

## § 4

Charles W. Chesnutt is a transitional figure. He drew together the various post-Civil War tendencies in Negro creative literature and translated them into the most worthy
prose fiction that the Negro had produced.

Chesnutt's career began with the publication of a series
of stories, starting in the *Atlantic Monthly* in 1887. In 1899
these stories were collected and issued as *The Conjure Woman*.
The book's reception as the work of a white writer indicates
much as to Chesnutt's earlier artistic objectivity and, more
important perhaps, signifies that he was judged by the standards of his white contemporaries. By these standards *The
Conjure Woman* is successful. In one stroke Chesnutt had
achieved what others had striven for interminably. Written
around a central framework, the care with which the stories
are done bespeaks the writer's artistic sincerity. The tales,
concerned with the deeds and misdeeds of a conjure woman,
are connected with each other in such a way as to give them
more than the superficial unity which the framework sup-
plies. The plan is very simple. Uncle Julius, a frosty-headed
Negro who has lived through and absorbed all the romance
and reality of slavery, tells the seven folk tales to a northern
white couple recently moved to North Carolina.

Though it was generally known that Chesnutt was a Negro
after the publication of *The Wife of His Youth* in 1899, he
nevertheless continued to write occasional stories that gave
no indication of his color. The satirical gem, "Baxter's Procustes," is the best known of these. But after a series of
stories and novels dealing with the Negro and the color line
and its problems, most of Chesnutt's objective stories seem
forced and unnatural, wan and vigorless, mere water colors.
For sheer accomplishment in work of this kind he never
surpassed *The Conjure Woman*, and none of his later stories
ever equaled the folk tale "The Gray Wolf's Ha'nt," that

dark and cruel tragedy of jealousy and love. Nearly all the stories of this first collection are tragic with the fatal consequences of human actions and prejudices. It is not the weak pseudo-tragedy of propaganda, it is not pathos and tears in which Chesnutt deals—it is the fundamental stuff of life translated into the folk terms of a people who knew true tragedy.

Chesnutt's first volume proved two important points. It proved that the Negro could be made the subject of serious esthetic treatment without the interference of propaganda; and it proved that the Negro creative artist could submerge himself objectively in his material. It must not be thought, however, that the tradition of buffoonery was broken by *The Conjure Woman*. The buffoon had two faces. He grinned and danced and capered as a minstrel Sambo and in the stories of certain popular authors, while Joel Chandler Harris saw the other face, the blandly kind and childish smile, the improvident generosity and loyalty. But he was still a Negro, lazy, ignorant, dependent. Both faces showed him as a woefully inferior being, and that was the very core of the tradition. Like a Jewish actor in pre-Christian Rome, he might be the instrument of tragedy, but he was never tragic. Beneath the mask there grinned the Negro.

After several years of teaching in North Carolina, Charles Chesnutt returned to his home in Cleveland in 1887. The effect upon him of his return to a way of life that had grown strange was immediate. In the South the distance between himself and the majority of Negroes with whom he came into contact was immeasurable. He was not wedded to them by the bonds of common circumstance, environment, and habit. He understood them, but he did not feel a blood-warm kinship to their earth, nor a destiny common to their destiny. The objectivity of *The Conjure Woman* argues the gulf. His sympathetic understanding of southern Negroes,

6

which never faltered, was in part at least the product of the very distance at which he stood from them. In Cleveland he was home again among the people of the color line, his people. He knew again the habits, problems, vagaries of life, his life, along the color line. Kinship here was real and inescapable. He had to shift his point of view, to feel the artist merge into the man. The title of his second book, *The Wife of his Youth and Other Stories of the Color Line*, is symptomatic. And when he appends the following to the story "The Web of Circumstance," we hear the soul cry of the Negro.

"We are told, when the cycle of years has rolled around, there is to be another golden age, when all men will dwell together in love and harmony—God speed the day . . . but give us here and there, and now and then, some little foretaste of this golden age, that we may the more patiently and hopefully await its coming."

The struggle between Chesnutt the artist and Chesnutt the man (not immediately resolved) is evident in *The Wife of His Youth*. In these stories Chesnutt discards folk material to deal with the lives of a certain Negro type in Cleveland, the "Groveland" of his stories. These people represent the special and important group of Negroes with a large admixture of white blood. Because the peculiar situation of the near-whites was (and is) considered ideal for the purposes of propaganda, their lives had been used by nearly all the Negro novelists prior to Dunbar. This put upon such characters a certain stamp, and in that stamp lay danger for Chesnutt the artist.

The moods in which Chesnutt approaches his material are puzzling. In only a few of these stories is the reader sure of the author's point of view, his convictions. In "A Matter of Principle," for an instance, a story of the color line in which the daughter of a well-to-do quadroon family loses a brilliant

marriage because her father mistakes a stout, black gentleman for the lover whom he has never seen—what is the
author's point of view? Based on the tragic absurdity of
colorphobia, the story is a comedy of manners in the Molière
sense. But what is Chesnutt's conviction as an artist? Does
he sympathize with the existence of a color caste within the
race? Is he holding his characters up to ridicule? Of what is
he trying to convince us? In this and other stories one seems
always at the point of making a discovery about the author,
but the discovery never matures. The truth seems to be that
in 1899, more than ten years after his return to Cleveland,
Chesnutt's struggle was still in progress. He still was not
sure what his attitude should be.

The title story, "The Wife of his Youth," is an exception.
The delicacy of its mood, the tempered sharpness of its
point, and the subtle simplicity of characterization remind
one of Hawthorne. Indeed, it might have been conceived
and executed by the author of *Twice Told Tales*. The story
is of a mulatto who, married to a dark-skinned Negro woman
as a very young man in slavery, escapes to the North, acquires an education, and forgets his black wife. After the
emancipation, in the midst of a celebration on the eve of
the mulatto's marriage to a woman of the color line, the
wife of his youth appears, and he acknowledges her before
the gathering of near-white friends. It is not character that
is of most interest here. The characters are flat, two-dimen-
sional. Situation, circumstance—and beyond these, the
whole complex social structure—draw our attention. Only
Chesnutt's brooding sympathy for the problems present in
the society of which he writes makes the story at all possible.
One feels here something more of his personality than that
which ordinarily belongs to creative writing. One finds here
a key to him, the ever-coiling spring of his future creative-
ness.

Whether written in the spirit of comedy or tragedy, all the stories in *The Wife of his Youth* deal with the entanglements resulting from miscegenation. They are stories of situation. They represent a new approach to the Negro character in fiction. They argue artistically and not too obviously (another was to do this later) of the way of life to which the Negro might attain were it not for the bugaboo of color. The picture of life which Chesnutt draws is not exaggerated. The Negro characters are simplified beyond any that had appeared other than as types in American fiction. This simplification and the fact that the characters are limited to a certain group makes them less than ever representative. But they are people. *The Wife of his Youth* thrust into Negro literature a brace of which it was sadly in need.

In his first novel, *The House Behind the Cedars*, Chesnutt the Negro emerges more distinctly outlined, with a greater consciousness of social kinship. This self-consciousness is seen nowhere more plainly than in the story material itself. Chesnutt had used the bi-racial elements in American life before, but he had put the Negro in the relationship of servant to the white master. No violence had been done the standard American concept. In an exploratory way he had reviewed the product of miscegenation. Now he was to probe the infinitely dark ways in which miscegenation worked. Without doing injustice to either racial group, he had to bring them together on a plane of intimacy never before attempted, save for purposes of propaganda, in American fiction. He succeeded remarkably well.

As in the shorter tales of the color line, *The House Behind the Cedars* is a situation story. Situation that does not develop from the inescapable strength or weakness, love or hate, weal or woe of character is likely to be too doctrinaire, and its assumptions much too general. Even when such stories avoid this danger, they are likely to become melodramatic.

Skillful and dispassionate handling is necessary to bring them safely between the rocky shore and the shoals. It is in this that Chesnutt shows his craftsmanship. The situation of Molly Waldon as the concubine of a white southern gentleman is not unusual. Relationships of this kind between Negro women and white men were pretty generally recognized. But the study of the circumstantial effects of Molly's *situation* upon her children was exceptional. When John and Rena cross the line into the white race and when George Tyron, the aristocratic scion of an old southern family, falls in love with Rena we come face to face with the immediate and personalized problem of race. All this happens through situation. But it is at this point that character, aided by Hardian twists of fate, comes in to play its part. Rena faces the same problem that faced Hardy's Tess—whether to disclose her secret (of Negro blood) on the chance that her happiness would not be destroyed thereby. Like Tess, she sees the problem as a moral issue. The Hardian flavor is strong : the primary sin which was, however, not her sin, the struggle between the desire for happiness and the propulsion to truth, the innumerable circumstances that work for and against, and finally the stark, bare tragedy and the resolution in death. For downright power, no novel of the Negro race quite equals *The House Behind the Cedars*.

Not the least important consideration in Chesnutt's first novel was the treatment of George Tyron. Numerous white writers, including George Cable, Thomas Dixon, and Mark Twain, had treated of love (of one sort or another) between black and white. But they followed the convention. They made such love always a degraded thing, a bestial thing, bitch and hound. Chesnutt manages differently. The relationship between Tyron and Rena is as free from moral turpitude as the love-life of goldfish. Even in the treatment of Molly Waldon's illegitimate love there is no sense of pruriency. The remarkable thing is that this decent conduct brings no shock as of the unreal or unnatural. Plausibility is not strained by it. In spite of the tradition, one accepts the idea of the probability without retching.

But beneath all the skillful management of character and situation one can feel the author losing the delicately balanced objectivity of his short stories. Sometimes it shows through the characters, through sharp thrusts of ironic dialogue, as when old Judge Straight is made to say to the quadroon boy, John Waldon, the son of his friend: "You are black, my lad, and you are not free. Did you ever hear of the Dred Scott decision, delivered by the great, wise, and learned Judge Taney?" Sometimes it shows in a direct address to the reader: "There are depths of fidelity and devotion in the Negro heart that have never been fathomed or fully appreciated. . . . Surely it were worth while to try some other weapon than scorn and contumely and hard words upon a people of our common race—the human race . . . for we are all children of a common Father, forget it as we may, and each one of us is in some measure his brother's keeper."

Chesnutt worked in hazardous elements—elements that in any moment of unawareness might prove his undoing.

In his second novel, *The Marrow of Tradition*, Chesnutt stumbled headlong into the dangers that had lurked for him in his earlier books. *The Marrow of Tradition* is definitely propaganda. All the reasonable sympathy, so marked in his previous books, and so necessary to fine artistic accomplishment, is gone. In a passion of hatred, he writes of insult, injustice, and ignorance, piling "scorn and contumely and hard words," not upon a situation, a way of life or thought, as he would have had perfect right to do, but upon the white race, "a people of our common race—the human race." Nothing of artistic sanity saves the novel from its melodramatic madness. Chesnutt no longer sees the white and the black with equal eye. He is no longer content to let the story tell itself or to let the characters live in the free air of their own inclinations. Possibility and probability find no kinship here; truth and reality are confused. Taking the race riot in 1899 in Wilmington, North Carolina (the "Wellington" of the novel), as the climax of his story, he fails to see that its reality encompasses the general truths to which he wishes to give voice no more than a monstrous production of the elements, an earthquake or a tornado, expresses the great truths of nature.

"A Negro had killed a white man,—the unpardonable sin, admitting neither excuse, justification, nor extenuation. From time immemorial it had been bred in the Southern white consciousness, and in the Negro consciousness also, for that matter, that the person of a white man was sacred from the touch of a Negro, no matter what the provocation. A dozen colored men lay dead in the streets of Wellington, inoffensive people, slain in cold blood because they had been bold enough to question the authority of those who had assailed them, or frightened enough to flee when they had been ordered to stand still; but their lives counted nothing against that of a riotous white man, who had courted death by attacking a body of armed men."

More delicately wrought is *The Colonel's Dream*, also a novel of purpose. It is a clear but partial exposition of the deadly social forces that were at that time at work in the South. It is tragic in the overwhelming defeat of the good intentions of Colonel Henry French. The Colonel represents for Chesnutt that modicum of intelligence and humane feeling to be found in every social situation. Colonel French returns to his southern home after many years in the North. His values have been modified. It is now his wish to destroy the social monster which he and others over long years have created. But he is helpless and finally hopeless before the hatred and the ignorance of the southern way of life. The "marrow," indeed the very backbone, "of tradition" blocks him on every hand. It prevents him from obtaining legal justice for the Negro; it bars him from bringing reason into the more common race relations; it even checks his fight against the inhumanity heaped upon the poor whites in the cotton mills. Tradition is too firmly entrenched, too big to fall before the petty strength of one man's idealism. In the end, broken, disillusioned, Colonel French gives up the fight and returns to the North.

Though in *The Marrow of Tradition* Chesnutt went as far back as *Clotelle* in mood and treatment, in his other works he brought Negro creative literature much further along. His early career was a great artistic success, for he did the one thing needful to the American Negro writer: he worked dangerous, habit-ridden material with passive calm and fearlessness. Considering more than the emotional factors that lay behind the American race problem, he exposed the Negro to critical analysis. Had he written a quarter of a century later his art would have gone far to solidify the frothy interest in the Negro aroused by *Nigger Heaven, Prancing Nigger, Porgy*, and the musical shows of Lew Leslie. No less can be said of him than has been already implied: he is the most solid representative of prose fiction that the Negro could boast before the 1920's, and even now his work in its kind has not been equaled.

§ 5

As early as 1880 a young "house father" at Hampton Institute had come to the conclusion that in a large degree unusual power of mind could be derived from training given the hands "in the process of mastering well three trades," and that "If one goes today into any Southern town, and asks for the leading and most reliable colored man in the community, I believe that in five cases out of ten he will be directed to a Negro who learned a trade during the days of slavery."[17]

Fifteen years later a tall, tawny Negro blinked his green-yellow eyes in the light of the Georgia sun, looked out over a sea of white faces and, as spokesman for ten millions of people, raised the outspread fingers of his hand above his head and spoke these words: "In all things that are purely social we can be as separate as the fingers, yet one as the hand in all things essential to mutual progress."[18]

But there was opposition to this statement of the fundamental hypothesis of racial inequality upon which the whole industrial-education-of-Negroes idea was founded:

"Herein lie buried many things which if read with patience may show the strange meaning of being black here at the dawn of the Twentieth Century. This meaning is not without interest to you, Gentle Reader; for the problem of the Twentieth Century is the problem of the color-line. . . ."

"Let the ears of a guilty people tingle with truth, and seventy millions sigh for the righteousness which exalteth nations, in this drear day when human brotherhood is a mockery and a snare."

Thus begins and ends a book, *The Souls of Black Folk*, published two years before Chesnutt's last novel and three years after Booker Washington's *Up From Slavery* began appearing serially in the *Outlook*. It was written by a man whose language burst fiery-red, disturbing, against the leaden background of the "Hampton idea." W. E. Burghardt Du-Bois, its author, saw in the policies of Booker Washington, the acknowledged leader of ten million black folk, merely the conversion of the minstrel Negro into a cornfield Negro who was still a minstrel, still, for all his labor and sweat, a buffoon. Dr. DuBois was protesting—and examining. He was indicating a complete severance with blind protest and misinformed propaganda. And he was bringing to his job one of the most thorough and brilliant minds of the day.

The struggle for ascendancy between the ideas expressed by these two men is a new phase of the old struggle between the liberal and the conservative. One, the conservative, preached dependence and through compromise an emergence into an economic, social and cultural stability never quite equal to the white man's. The other, the liberal, preached courageous independence, a fight to obtain without compromise such rights and privileges as belonged to members of the civilization of which he was a part. The conservative accepted the immediate: the liberal peered with narrowed eyes into the future. Booker Washington was governed by the traditions of the South. Dr. DuBois was trained in the liberal institutions of Europe and was a graduate of Harvard.

So far as the permanent results to Negro literature are concerned, the struggle was one-sided from the beginning. The Negro was tired of compromise. Booker Washington, though he spoke from a thousand platforms and wrote a million words, spoke almost exclusively to whites who, unchallenged, had set him up as the leader of his people. He did not speak the words Negroes wanted to hear. Had he done so, his standing among whites as the chief of Negroes would have come to an end. It is amazing to find that he did not influence toward conservative thinking a single Negro writer of importance. On the other hand, Dr. DuBois was the very head and front of the Negro's newer liberalism. Though with the exception of *The Souls of Black Folk* and *The Quest of the Silver Fleece* his early career was devoted to scholarly sociological writing, he gave substance and form to the vague and troubling emotions, the ideals of race consciousness, race pride, and race culture which the Negroes wanted expressed. His "Credo" delivers up the essence of the man and shows that quality which made him attractive to his race:

"I believe in God, who made of one blood all nations that on earth do dwell. I believe that all men, black, brown, and white, are brothers, varying through time and opportunity, in form and gift and feature, but differing in no essential particular, and alike in soul and the possibility of infinite development.

"Especially do I believe in the Negro race: in the beauty of its genius, the sweetness of its soul, and its strength in that meekness which shall yet inherit this turbulent earth. I believe in pride of race and lineage and self: in pride of self so deep as to scorn injustice to other selves; in pride of lineage so great as to despise no man's father; in pride of race so chivalrous as neither to offer bastardy to the weak nor beg wedlock of the strong, knowing that men may be brothers in Christ, even though they be no brothers-in-law."[19]

This is the language of the inspired leader who, after 1910, month after month thundered in righteous wrath through the pages of the *Crisis* magazine and *Darkwater* and *The Dark Princess*. Long before taking up his editorial duties, however, Dr. DuBois had clarified his objectives as no other Negro writer had done. In a large measure all of his earlier work was clarification. The *Suppression of the African Slave Trade*, still the standard work on this subject, marked his entrance into Negro material. The study and research done in preparation of *The Negro in Philadelphia* gave him that intimate knowledge of the practical problems with which the Negro masses had to contend. *The Souls of Black Folk* is the first product of his combined thinking and feeling. It is in this book that he grows to fullness as a writer, fusing into a style that is beautifully lucid the emotional power that later made his *Crisis* editorials unsurpassed by any writing of their kind.

"I sit with Shakespeare and he winces not. Across the color line I move arm in arm with Balzac and Dumas, where smiling men and welcoming women glide in gilded halls. From out the caves of evening that swing between the strong-limbed earth and the tracery of the stars, I summon Aristotle and Aurelius and what soul I will, and they come all graciously with no scorn nor condescension. So, wed with Truth, I dwell before the Veil. Is this the life you grudge us, O knightly America? Is this the life you long to change into the dull red hideousness of Georgia? Are you so afraid lest peering from this high Pisgah, between Philistine and Amalekite, we sight the Promised Land?"[20]

A combination of scholarship and emotional power woven into bolts of symbolism characterize Dr. DuBois's writing. Only Carlyle stands comparison. The welded elements of Dr. DuBois's style enabled him to set forth ideas in a language which aroused feeling. What has been said of Carlyle has also been said of him: "Even when I do not understand him, I know his meaning." This power of setting forth the abstract concretely is the rarest gift of all. It was a gift indispensable to the full effectiveness of Dr. DuBois's later career. From 1909, the year of his biography *John Brown*, he was an avowed propagandist, setting himself the task of remolding the destiny of a race. It is doubtful that from that time forward he considered himself a literary artist in the strict sense of the term. This is not to say that he smothered his appreciation for the esthetic qualities of his medium. But he did not hoodwink himself that propaganda could successfully masquerade as art. He continued to write with the craftsman's care and sensitiveness that has made him a master of English prose style, but toward ends that were utilitarian.

Dr. DuBois's first novel, *The Quest of the Silver Fleece*, is entirely in keeping with the purpose he had set himself. It is not a novel so much as it is fact fictionized. It differs from run-of-the-mine Negro propaganda in that it seeks to impress the mind by a reasonable exposition of facts concerning the economic status of the southern Negro. In it he did not speak as forcefully "both to our spirits and our intellects" as in the later novel, *Dark Princess*. This last is a strange book, a strange compound of revolutionary doctrine and futilistic philosophy, refuting, it seems, Dr. DuBois's own text of aggressive independence. Matthew Towns, the main character, lives between two worlds as between grinding millstones : above him is the world of the whites, below him the world of the blacks. And where he lives there is futility, the utter and ironic waste of life symbolized so movingly in the suicide of Perigua, the Indian who also lived between two worlds. Contrasted with these are those Negroes characterized by what Allison Davis calls their "meanness of spirit," who maintain their security and comfort by "truckling"—again to quote Davis—"to the white world of power, and exploiting the common Negro." Perigua delineates them : " 'We're so glad to have a white man fling us swill that we wiggle on our bellies and crawl. We slave that they may loll; we hand over our daughters to be their prostitutes. We're afraid, we're scared; we're congenital idiots and cowards. Don't tell me, you fool. Your caution is cowardice inbred for ten generations; you want to talk, talk, talk and argue until somebody in pity and contempt gives you what you dare not take'."

And for both the Matthew Townses and the mean-of-spirit, life is a barren waste. There is an unwholesome sanity, a poisonous power in the book. It calls for mithridatic stomachs.

But it is through his essays and editorials that Dr. DuBois

has wielded his greatest influence upon Negro thought and letters. For more than a decade from 1903 through the death of Booker Washington until 1917 the Negro was leashed between the contrary opinions of DuBois and Washington. There was apparent deadlock. Excepting the work of Washington and DuBois there were very few important books by Negroes published during those fourteen years. A few poems on unracial themes were published from time to time in important periodicals. But Negro writers seemed to have gone sterile. Washington of course easily found publishers. There was no lack of writers who were greater craftsmen than he, and had they chosen to work in similar material they, too, would have found publishers. Negro intellectuals just were not believing in Washington. The work of these intellectuals, inspired by the liberalism of DuBois, conformed to no racial pattern acceptable to the white public. They spoke nothing to America because America would not hear. Courageous publishers were scarce. As far as white America cared to know, there was but one Negro writer, and all he demanded of his audience was a few dollars, an occasional pat on the back, and an otherwise passive acceptance. And all this time Dr. DuBois was writing essays and editorials for black consumption.

So the deadlock was only apparent. Williams and Walker, Cole and Johnson, and other famous vaudeville and minstrel troupes might cavort to the coon songs of Rosamond Johnson on the stages of white theaters, but death was upon them. Dixon might write *The Clansman* and *The Leopard's Spots;* Blease and Vardaman might grind out their anathemas; Nearing, Pollard, and Carpenter might try to preserve by scientific abracadabra the belief that the Negro was inherently an inferior being, but they were powerless to hold back one tittle the tremendous intellectual and spiritual force that was generating against the bulwarks of popular conception.

The great tradition was passing. Its passing was heralded in the *Crisis* and the Afro-American press generally, whose pages were eloquent with the tongues of liberals. Material of all sorts poured into the clean, new channels of liberalism—sociology, biology, anthropology, education, religion, criticism, poetry, prose fiction. The Afro-American press was a sort of testing hopper in which the new ideas could be tried and stored until the time was ripe to bring them forth into the light of the white world. In the very van of this activity, the light of apostolic sincerity on his brow, was Dr. DuBois, writing, writing, writing. He wrote : "It took but a few years of Atlanta to bring me to hot and indignant defense. I saw the race-hatred of the whites as I had never dreamed of it before,—naked and unashamed! The faint discrimination of my hopes and intangible dislikes paled into nothing before this great, red monster of cruel oppression."[21]

He wrote : "This assumption that of all the hues of God whiteness alone is inherently and obviously better than brownness or tan leads to curious acts ; even the sweeter souls of the dominant worlds as they discourse with me on weather, weal, and woe are continually playing above their actual words an obligato of tune and tone, saying : 'My poor, un-white thing! Weep not nor rage. I know, too well, that the curse of God lies heavy on you. Why? That is not for me to say, but be brave! Do your work in your lowly sphere, praying the good Lord that into heaven above, where all is love, you may, one day, be born—white!' "[22]

He wrote : "The present problem of problems is nothing more than democracy beating itself helplessly against the color bar,—purling, seeping, seething, foaming to burst

through, ever and again overwhelming the emerging masses
of white men in its rolling backwaters and held back by
those who dream of future kingdoms of greed built on black
and brown and yellow slavery.''[23]

He wrote :

> I hate them, Oh!
> I hate them well,
> I hate them, Christ!
> As I hate hell!
> If I were God,
> I'd sound their knell
> This day!
> Who raised the fools to their glory,
> But black men of Egypt and Ind,
> Ethiopia's sons of the evening,
> Indians and yellow Chinese,
> Arabian children of the morning,
> And mongrels of Rome and Greece?[24]

In 1920 appeared *Darkwater*, a collection of essays, editorials, poems, and sketches. Most of the pieces which make
up the volume had been written years before, during the
restless time of generation and uncertainty. In a large measure they had served their purpose, but in 1920 they were
offered to the world at large because the world had been
made somewhat ready to receive them. Various of them,
foretimed, had appeared in the *Atlantic Monthly* and the
*Independent*, but most of them had been published in the
*Crisis*. They represent the greatness of Dr. DuBois as an
inspirational force. They represent in little his directive significance to Negro creative literature. But aside from this,
there are six poems in *Darkwater* which make the volume
even more notable. They are the only poems he has ever
published, though his career is not yet done. Like his best

prose, these lyric chants have a poisonous and bitter beauty, the gravity of symbolism.

O Silent God, Thou whose voice afar in mist and
mystery hath left our ears an-hungered in these
fearful days—
               Hear us, good Lord!

.         .         .         .         .         .         .

Wherefore do we pray? Is not the God of Fathers
dead? Have not seers seen in Heaven's halls thine
hearsed and lifeless form stark amidst the black and
rolling smoke of sin, where all along bow bitter
forms of endless dead?
               Awake, Thou that sleepest!

.         .         .         .         .         .         .

   Forgive us, good Lord : we know not
what we say!

Bewildered we are and passioned-tossed, mad with
the madness of a mobbed and mocked and mur-
dered people ; straining at the armposts of Thy
throne, we raise our shackled hands and charge
Thee, God, by the bones of our stolen fathers, by
the tears of our dead mothers, by the very blood of
the crucified Christ : what meaneth this? Tell us
the plan : give us the sign!
               Keep not Thou silent, O God![25]

## § 6

The years from 1903 to 1917 mark a gap in the continuity
of creative drive and purpose in the works of those Negro
writers whose talents earned them the hearing of the general

7

public. This can be accounted for in only one way: during the intense struggle between liberal and conservative the Negro was taking stock, weighing opinions, and awaiting with bated breath the collapse of the gates through which he could pass into his creative freedom. In general the Negro felt that the larger public of white America was not ready for the new ideas, was not prepared to accept the new Negro he felt he had become. Here and there attempts were made to hasten the day of enlightenment, but they were as forewarning sparks of a general conflagration. Three volumes, *A Little Dreaming, Visions of the Dusk,* and *Songs of the Soil,* by Fenton Johnson are of this nature.

It is probably through Fenton Johnson that the influence of the midwestern poets, Lindsay, Sandburg, and Masters, first touched Negro writers. Johnson himself was born and educated in Chicago. Like the white Chicago group, he contributed to *Others* and to *Poetry, A Magazine of Verse.* Like them, too, he wrote free verse on subjects that were the particular grist of the poets of the Chicago "golden era." He wrote of frustrated hopes, "the easiest way," of streetwalkers, ditchdiggers, saloon roustabouts.

> Once I was good like the Virgin Mary and the
>     minister's wife.
> My father worked for Mr. Pullman and white
>     people's tips;
> But he died two days after his insurance expired.
> I had nothing, so I had to go to work.
> All the stock I had was a white girl's education and
>     a face that enchanted the men of both races.
> Starvation danced with me.
> So when Big Lizzie, who kept a house for white men,
>     came to me with tales of fortune that I could

reap from the sale of my virtue I bowed my head
to Vice.
Now I can drink more gin than any man for miles
around.
Gin is better than all the water in Lethe.[26]

The similarity of some of the pieces of Langston Hughes
to certain of Johnson's is striking, but the point must not be
labored, for in general they differ widely. Essentially, Johnson was a despairing poet, stuffed with the bitterness of Du-
Bois. The attitude of despair, common among the early
"New Negroes," in Johnson's case is ineffectually sustained.
The lines,

> Throw the children into the river; civilization has
> given us too many of them. It is better to die
> than it is to grow up and find out you're
> colored,[27]

are supported neither by strong emotion nor apt expression.
They are false to the emotion of despair as the Negro feels
it, and run counter to an essential quality of spirit. Johnson
was more nearly race-expressive when he wrote :

> We are the star-dust folk,
>     Striving folk!
> Sorrow songs have lulled to rest
> Seething passions wrought through wrongs,
> Led us where the moon rays dip
> In the night of dull despair,
> Showed us where the star-gleams shine.[28]

But Fenton Johnson's poetry, like James Weldon Johnson's novel, *The Autobiography of an Ex-Colored Man*, foreran

its time. The reception accorded these men as writers of
Negro literature of a serious vein was more than cool : it was
downright freezing. That their failure to arouse interest was
not due to any lack of creative talent is proved by the fact
that both of them published pieces of considerable merit in
first-rate literary journals of the day, and by the inclusion
of some of their early work in recent anthologies. It was
theme and spirit with which America would have nothing
to do. The young James Weldon Johnson might write "My
City" with the assurance of publication in the *Century*, whose
editor was Richard W. Gilder :

When I come down to sleep death's endless night,
The threshold of the unknown dark to cross,
What to me then will be the keenest loss,
When this bright world blurs on my fading sight?
Will it be that no more I shall see the trees
Or smell the flowers or hear the singing birds
Or watch the flashing streams of patient herds?
No, I am sure it will be none of these.

But, ah! Manhattan's sights and sounds, her smells,
Her crowds, her throbbing force, the thrill that comes
From being of her a part, her subtile spells,
Her shining towers, her avenues, her slums—
O God! the stark, unutterable pity,
To be dead, and never again behold my city![29]

But from 1903 to 1917 there was no place for these, though
Brander Matthews himself might praise them :

For never let the thought arise
That we are here on sufferance bare ;
Outcasts, asylumed 'neath these skies.
And aliens without part or share.

This land is ours by right of birth,
This land is ours by right of toil;
We helped to turn its virgin earth;
Our sweat is in its fruitful soil.

Then should we speak but servile words,
Or shall we hang our heads in shame?
Stand back of new-come foreign hordes,
And fear our heritage to claim?[30]

The world beyond the walled world of Negro life was not
ready, and after a few sporadic attempts to shout the world
into attention, Negro writers for the public at large perforce
directed their energies toward work of another kind. The
involuntary hiatus in the purposeful drive of creative energies was complete. Kinless verse of the type of James Weldon
Johnson's "My City" was effectively done by any number
of Negro poets. George Marion McClellan, for an instance,
was an entirely conventional nature poet, a poet of green
fields, and low hills, and laughing water. Alice Dunbar,
Angelina Grimke, Sara Fleming, and Joseph Cotter wrote
tidy lyrics in the conventional manner on conventional
themes. And at least one Negro writer, William Stanley
Braithwaite, attained prominence as critic and anthologist.
His leading reviews for the *Boston Transcript*, his anthologies
of magazine verse, published yearly from 1913 to 1928, and
a collection of Elizabethan verse mark him as a critic of
great sensibility. Braithwaite's poetry, however, is of greater
pertinence to this study. He is the most outstanding example
of perverted energy that the period from 1903 to 1917 produced.

Various explanations have been given for the oddity which
a study of certain Negro poets like Braithwaite presents,
but not one takes into account the pressure of the age. It is

not considered that the expression of certain thoughts, feelings, and ideas was denied if they wished the hearing of an important audience. No one of the explanations mentions that all but one of these poets wrote better verse on material that in the very nature of things was (rather than is) Negro material. Braithwaite is the exception. On this general head, Countee Cullen has something to say in the preface to *Caroling Dusk:* "Since theirs [Negro writers] is also the heritage of the English language, their work will not present any serious aberration from the poetic tendencies of their time . . . for the double obligation of being both Negro and American is not so unified as we are often led to believe." Also, and apparently by way of explanation, Braithwaite's autobiographical sketch has this to say : "I inherited the incentives and ideals of the intellect from an ancestry of British gentlemen."[31] Further, it might be pointed out that he was born in Boston and has lived most of his life in Massachusetts. These remarks are definitely offered in the nature of excuses for divergence from the racial norm of creative ends.

Most of the Negro poets who from nearly the beginning of the century to the middle years of the World War turned their talents toward traditional poetic material—love, birth, death, beauty, grief, gladness—without any thought of their racial background developed a sort of dilettantism, a kind of love of display of poetic skill, and experience, and knowledge. In this their verse is comparable to the tricky poetics of the Cavaliers. It is bright and light, but without substance —Chinese fireworks.

> Lolotte, who attires my hair,
> Lost her lover. Lolotte weeps ;
> Trails her hand before her eyes ;
> Hangs her head and mopes and sighs,

Mutters of the pangs of hell.
Fills the circumambient air
With her plaints and her despair.
Looks at me :
"May you never know, Mam'selle,
Love's harsh cruelty."[32]

Now this is pretty and skillful poetry, but it is not poetry afire with the compelling necessity for expression. No passion (even slightly remembered in tranquillity) of pain or joy, no spring of pure personal knowledge or conviction justifies it. It is just "lines expressing something or other."

Mr. Braithwaite set the pace for this particular school. It is not enough, however, to say that he seems to be merely a dilettante. He is both much more and much less than that— but it is not quite clear what or how much. In the *Poetic Year* for 1916, he wrote : "All this life that we live, this experience that we have of the world, are but footnotes to reality. . . . Ever since the beginning man has tried to translate the language of the spirit—the invisible, immaterial character of another existence that is as real as our own." Despite his brave, plain words, his translation of the language of the spirit leaves much to be desired in the way of clarity, and he seems never to have understood the "footnotes to reality." His poems mark the path of his steady progress into the rare atmosphere of the spiritual world, until at last he wrote "Sandy Star and Willie Gee," a poem in five titled parts, exclusive of the introduction :

Sandy Star and Willie Gee
Count 'em two, you make 'em three :
Pluck the man and boy apart
And you'll see into my heart.

### III

### Exit

No, his exit by the gate
    Will not leave the wind ajar;
He will go when it is late
    With a misty star.

### v

### Onus Probandi

No more from out the sunset,
    No more across the foam,
No more across the windy hills
    Will Sandy Star come home.

He went away to search it
    With a curse upon his tongue
And in his hand the staff of life
    Made music as it swung.

I wonder if he found it,
    And knows the mystery now—
Our Sandy Star who went away
    With the secret on his brow.[33]

And none but a few of the now declined esoteric cult understood him.

# 4. *Emergence of the New Negro*

CLAUDE MCKAY, JEAN TOOMER, JESSIE FAUSET, LANG-
STON HUGHES, COUNTEE CULLEN, RUDOLPH FISHER,
JAMES WELDON JOHNSON, AND OTHERS

§ I

By the time of the death of Booker Washington in 1915 the
Negro, with Dr. DuBois as chief architect, had reared a
complicated thought structure designed as impregnable
against the shifting circumstances of that day. He was certain that he must assimilate the characteristics of white
America, while at the same time he took pride in his own
peculiar contribution to American civilization. He earnestly
wished to develop a culture within a culture at the same
time laughing derisively at those who urged a forty-ninth
state for the colonization of Negroes. Whenever possible he
ignored all consciousness of race, and yet he crowded into
third-class accommodations for which he had paid first-
class rates, cluttered up the segregated balconies of theaters,
and made it a point of pride whenever he was accepted on
the same terms as any other citizen. Negroes went to Harvard, Yale, Chicago, and fought for entrance into Bryn
Mawr, and yet defended to exhaustion their avowals that
Howard, Lincoln, and Spelman were "just as good." When
a Negro married a white woman it was reason for jubilant
comment, but a Negro girl's step across the line cost her
family, friends, and reputation. One system of thought
operated for the group ; another for the individual.

All this was in the direction of adjustment. That in the
beginning it was so inconsistent was because the serious
effort was all on the part of the Negro, and within the group.
The revolving wheel of the Negro's thought could find no
firm traction on the surface of white America's conscious-

ness. Change came haltingly. Since the publication of Ray Stannard Baker's *Following the Color Line* in 1908 there had been a sporadic interest among southern whites in the deeper problems of race relations. The list of books about Negroes grew, and the items became more studious. For the most part, however, the country slumbered in Booker Washington's belief that the problem of race could be solved by erecting agricultural and mechanical schools and colleges for Negroes.

Then came the war in Europe. Thousands of foreign laborers, German, Italian, French, Austrian, were recalled. By early 1915 there was a serious labor shortage. The steel, munitions, and automotive industries in Pittsburgh and Carney's Point, Detroit and Tom's River were forced to cancel contracts they could not fill because hands were short. Prices and wages advanced. Industry sent representatives South to shark up labor. That spring the agricultural South had been hard hit first by flood and then by drouth, and hundreds of the Negro population were idle. Others, the floaters and transients in normal days, were attracted by the high wages offered by the northern industrialists. In the five years from 1915 to 1920 a half million Negroes moved North.[1]

The effect of this first great Negro migration upon the thought of white America was tremendous. In the South there was alarm that its labor supply would be seriously curtailed, effecting a breakdown in the agricultural trades, and especially in cotton. The first reaction was toward unhealthy repressive measures, but this soon gave way to an intelligent appraisal. For the first time since the Civil War the whole mind of the South was aware that the Negro was a free agent; that he suffered economic exploitation only when he could not help himself, and that, like any other people, he moved toward greater opportunities. The new sociological interest in the Negro in the South was reflected in the increase in books on racial relations written from the southern point of view. They began to pour from the press. All of these were not temperate, but the majority were a distinct victory of mind over prejudice.

In the North the effect was no less telling. The North was getting a full measure of the race problem in industry and in such social problems as housing, health, education, and crime. Detroit, Pittsburgh, Chicago, Philadelphia, and scores of smaller cities saw rises of from 40 to 140 per cent in their Negro populations. Such increases demanded new adjustments on both sides. Not only (to paraphrase the title of one of the books of the period) was the Negro facing America, but America was facing the Negro. America at large was sociology-minded. Various cities engaged experts to work on the problems incident to the Negro. Social agencies established departments of Negro work. Negro organizations of local and national significance came into being for the specific purpose of bettering race relations. No longer did a few social-minded patrons and philanthropic titans limit the white race's actions and attitudes in regard to America's most absorbing problem, to the giving of money for the maintenance of inferior schools.

The Negro felt the strength of the new and vigorous interest more powerfully than he had felt the effects of the Civil War. Both a party to and subject of a multitude of studies, he was at no loss for want of a general attitude. The psychology of oppression by which he was dominated and to which he had given expression in apologetic language, defeatist poetry, and apostate prose controlled him still, though now it began boldly to express itself in harangues and declarations. Now that America had by its own will been made ready to listen, the Negro began that revelation and vindication of himself, that impassioned study of his accomplishments, that declaration of his future that creates the masculine literature of the "New Negro."

In 1910 James Weldon Johnson had been content to pray, although with strength, humbly :

> God of our weary years,
> God of our silent tears,
> Thou who hast brought us thus far on our way ;
> Thou who hast by thy might
> Led us into the light,
> Keep us ever in the path, we pray.
> Lest our feet stray from the places, our God,
>     where we met Thee ;
> Lest our hearts, drunk with the wine of the world,
>     we forget Thee :
> Shadowed beneath Thy hand,
> May we forever stand,
> True to our God,
> True to our native land.[2]

But in 1917, in the title poem of his volume *Fifty Years*, he declared :

> Far, far the way that we have trod
>     From heathen kraal and jungle dens,
> To freedmen, freemen, sons of God,
>     Americans and citizens.
>
> .    .    .    .    .
>
> A few black bondmen strewn along
>     The borders of our eastern coast,
> Now grown a race ten million strong,
>     An upward, onward, marching host.

Then should we speak but servile words,
Or shall we hang our heads in shame?
Stand back of new-come foreign hordes,
And fear our heritage to claim?

No! stand erect and without fear,
And for our foes let this suffice—
We've bought a rightful kinship here
And we have more than paid the price.

These were not the words of a passionate inexperienced youth. At the time they were written Mr. Johnson was forty-five; he had been teacher, lawyer, and United States Consul at Venezuela and Nicaragua. Next to Dr. DuBois, he understood the temper of his own people and the prevailing attitude of the whites better than any Negro of the day.

*Fifty Years* is not an isolated instance. Between 1917 and 1921 other Negro writers followed Mr. Johnson's lead. Waverly Carmichael, Joshua Jones, and Leslie P. Hill published volumes that had comparatively wide sales among both Negroes and whites. For the most part the work of these men was largely preparatory and gave but faint promise of the skill of the writers who were to crown the era of revival. Things of broad social consequence were happening too fast to permit utter concentration upon art. The return of American soldiers to the United States seems to have been a signal for a series of disturbances of wide significance. Causes were not far to seek. Negroes had not only replaced depleted foreign labor in the years prior to America's entrance into the war, but they had been used in many skilled capacities formerly filled by whites. In the North it was no longer general to refer to certain jobs as "white" jobs. Competition between Negroes and whites (and especially the returned soldiers of both groups) for these jobs in industry was one cause. Another cause, no less potent, was the attitude of the Negroes themselves. They had fought "to make the world safe for democracy" and they wanted to share in the benefits of democracy. Julia Johnson in *The Negro Problem* notes that Dr. DuBois commented : "Under similar circumstances we would fight again. But, by the God of Heaven, we are cowards and jackasses if, now that the war is over, we do not marshal every ounce of our brain and brawn to fight a sterner, longer, more unbending battle against the forces of hell in our own land."

And Rollin Harte, who coined the term "New Negro," had this to say : "Here [is] the same spirit—the spirit, that is, of the new Negro. Hit, he hits back. In a succession of race riots, he has proved it. 'When they taught the colored boys to fight,' says a Negro newspaper, 'they started something they won't be able to stop'. . . . That huge, leaderless exodus . . . meant for the first time in his history the Negro had taken affairs into his own hands. Until then, things had been done to the Negro, with the Negro, and for the Negro, but never by the Negro. At last he showed initiative and self-reliance."[3]

There were bloody, costly riots in Chester, Washington, Chicago, and East St. Louis. The attitude of the race was reflected by the first important poet of the black renaissance, Claude McKay, in "If We Must Die" :

Oh, Kinsmen! We must meet the common foe ;
  Though far outnumbered, let us still be brave,
And for their thousand blows deal one death blow!
  What though before us lies the open grave?
Like men we'll face the murderous, cowardly pack,
  Pressed to the wall, dying, but fighting back![4]

§ 2

Out of these conditions grew a new sanity on both sides, a new respect for the hidden powers of each, and a desire to come together in a spirit of mutual helpfulness. The Chicago Commission on Race Relations, appointed in 1919, created the guides by which interracial conferences have been held ever since. Gradually, as the bugaboo of the Negro as an agent of social destruction was exorcised, America began to look at her dark citizens for powers of positive good. She began to appraise the Negro folk songs and the spirituals (long popularized by singers from Fisk University and Hampton Institute), poetry, painting, and art. From 1919 to the present this interest has not slackened. It has found expression in the material of graduate theses, in sociological tracts, in magazine articles. It has added piquancy to moving pictures and the musical comedy stage. It has served Eugene O'Neill, Paul Green, and Marc Connelly in the drama; DuBose Heyward, Carl Van Vechten, Roark Bradford, Sherwood Anderson, and dozens of lesser writers in the novel; Virgil Thompson and Gershwin in music; and Lindsay and Sandburg in poetry.

Since the war Negro artists had been producing and awaiting a ripe time. Had they been left much longer to feed upon the interest that they as artists stimulated in their own group, their efforts would have petered out. An audience within the Negro group was not sufficiently large to support them, and consequently there could have been no profits for potential distributing agencies that might have handled the work of the writers. Of the two Negro publishing firms established between 1915 and 1922 for the purpose of issuing books by Negroes about Negroes,[5] one had to beg funds for its existence and the other was forced to close. To a much greater extent then than now, Negro writers had to depend upon the will of white America. In about 1921, fortunately, America's interest in the Negro as he expressed himself was outrun only by her interest in expressing the Negro. In a very large measure this constitutes what has been called the Negro renaissance. James Weldon Johnson in "The Dilemma of the Negro Author" has this to say: "What has happened is that efforts which have been going on for more than a century are being noticed and appreciated at last, and that this appreciation has served as a stimulus to greater effort and output. . . . Several converging forces have been at work."[6]

That the Negro was stimulated to greater creative effort by the interest of white America is beyond doubt. It is remarkable, however, that his semi-dependent position as an artist (and especially as a writer) did not lead him in most instances into the production merely of what the white man wanted. Black and white America had come a long way in the two decades since 1900. Though there was still in the attitude of white America something of the playful indulgence of a giant for a pigmy, there rose up important numbers of critics and readers like Robert Kerlin, Waldo Frank, Paul Rosenfeld, Louis Untermeyer, V. F. Calverton, Joel Spingarn, and Henry Mencken who were sincere and strong in their belief that the Negro writer had a particular gift to make to American culture.

It was to the sincerity of these men and to the devotion and encouragement of their own small racial audience that Negro writers tied. The discipline of their virtual silence in the war years had been good for them. The traditions which would have limited their appeal had atrophied; popular concepts were topsy-turvy. A truly *new* Negro had been born and grown into maturity during the years since 1900. He was a breathing amalgam of numerous tendencies. He was race conscious and race proud, independent and defiant, conscious of his powers and not ashamed of his gifts. He came without apology and meaning no offense, but ready to defend himself when offense was taken. His position as an artist was exactly reversed from that of most of his predecessors. He lived and worked for his own people and discovered to his astonishment that by satisfying them he pleased also a vast but incidental white audience. He was not immediately a pioneer in new forms, for he was just beginning to fix his own artistic values, but the reception he got for being *new* and *different* encouraged him to think that at long last he was a part of America's cultural life.

The new Negro movement in literature began with a West Indian Negro. Claude McKay had already published a few dialect pieces[7] when he came to the States in 1912, drifting from Tuskegee to Kansas and on to New York. His first years in New York were concurrent with the early social thinking that had been stimulated by reason of the war. Working in an editorial capacity for the *Liberator* and *The Masses*, he must have felt the liberal currents that swept through the pages of those journals ; but his infrequent poems gave no hint of his own social thinking. Even the volume *Spring in New Hampshire* reveals more of the conservative poet of nature than of the bitter revolutionary of a few months later. But his gifts stand out in that volume—his love of color, his lush imagery, his sensitive massing. The sometimes indefinable difference that marks the work of the new Negro writer is evident throughout *Harlem Shadows* and especially in such pieces as "Harlem Shadows," "The Harlem Dancer," and "The Tropics in New York."

> Bananas ripe and green, and ginger root,
> Cocoa in pods and alligator pears,
> And tangerines and mangoes and grape fruit,

Fit for the highest prize at parish fairs,
Sat in the window, bringing memories
  Of fruit-trees laden by low-singing rills,
And dewy dawns, and mystical blue skies
  In benediction over nun-like hills.

My eyes grew dim and I could no more gaze;
  A wave of longing through my body swept,
And, hungry for the old familiar ways,
  I turned aside and bowed my head and wept.[8]

It was Mr. McKay's third volume of poetry, *Harlem Shad-ows*, that attracted his darker audience most. In this volume he gives voice to the violence and bitter hatred that marked the interracial strife of the period just after the war. The proud defiance and independence that were the very heart of the new Negro movement is nowhere so strikingly expressed in poetry as in "To the White Fiends" and in "If We Must Die," already quoted.

Despite the awakening of a new artistic consciousness, however, there was at first much confusion in the new Negro movement in literature. The great tide of feeling which found release was not directed through one channel. While Claude McKay spat out his proud impatience, a few were indulging in slapstick, trying in song and story (and with the aid of certain popular white writers) to restore the older tradition to a state of health, and other writers were groping with curious shyness through the teeming byways of racial thought and feeling, searching for an alchemy, a universal solvent for transmuting the passions of the day into something sweeter than bitterness, more pure than hate. They were for the most part older writers who had an hereditary confidence in the essential goodness of man, in the theory of American democracy, and in the Victorian notion that

God's in his heaven;
All's right with the world.

They were of the comfortable middle classes, the bourgeois, school teachers, the wives of pork-fattened politicians and ministers, the sons of headwaiters and porters, spiritually far removed from the sources of new race thought. McKay, Toomer, Hughes, and the numerous lesser ones who came later were vagabonds, as free in the sun and dust of Georgia, in the steerage of tramp steamers, in the brothels of Lenox Avenue and the crowded ports of the Orient as in the living rooms of Strivers Row. These were the reservoirs through which pumped the race's hate power, love power, lust power, laugh power. The others, the conservatives, were tubs without depth, within whose narrow limits no storm could be raised. They posed themselves questions: Am I not just as well as I am? Must I be proud and glory in my race? And they sought to answer them.

> We ask for peace. We, at the bound
> Of life, are weary of the round
> In search of Truth. We know the quest
> Is not for us, the vision blest
> Is meant for other eyes. Uncrowned,
> We go, with heads bowed to the ground,
> And old hands, gnarled and hard and browned.
> Let us forget the past unrest,—
>      We ask for peace.[9]

> We will not waver in our loyalty.
> No strange voice reaches us across the sea :
> No crime at home shall stir us from this soil.
> Ours is the guerdon, ours the blight of toil,
> But raised above it by a faith sublime
> We choose to suffer here and bide our time.[10]

But the bourgeois could not restrain the flood tide. In 1923 came Jean Toomer's *Cane*, a revolutionary book that gave definiteness to the new movement and exposed a wealth of new material. A youth of twenty-eight fresh from the South when *Cane* was published, he held nothing so important to the artistic treatment of Negroes as racial kinship with them. Unashamed and unrestrained, Jean Toomer loved the race and the soil that sustained it. His moods are hot, colorful, primitive, but more akin to the naïve hysteria of the spirituals than to the sophisticated savagery of jazz and the blues. *Cane* was a lesson in emotional release and freedom. Through all its prose and poetry gushes a subjective tide of love. "He comes like a son returned in bare time to take a living full farewell of a dying parent; and all of him loves and wants to commemorate that perishing naïvete."[11] Hear how he revels in the joy and pain, the beauty and tragedy of his people :

> Pour, O pour that parting soul in song,
> O pour it in the sawdust glow of night,
> Into the velvet pine-smoke air tonight,
> And let the valley carry it along.
> And let the valley carry it along.
>
> O land and soil, red soil and sweet-gum tree,
> So scant of grass, so profligate of pines,
> Now just before an epoch's sun declines,
> Thy son, in time, I have returned to thee,
> Thy son, I have in time returned to thee.
>
> In time, for though the sun is setting on
> A song-lit race of slaves, it has not set ;
> Though late, O soil, it is not too late yet
> To catch thy plaintive soul, leaving, soon gone,
> Leaving, to catch thy plaintive soul soon gone.

O Negro slaves, dark purple ripened plums,
Squeezed, and bursting in the pine-wood air,
Passing, before they stripped the old tree bare
One plum was saved for me, one seed becomes

An everlasting song, a singing tree,
Caroling softly souls of slavery,
What they were, and what they are to me,
Caroling softly souls of slavery.[12]

Great splotches of color and sensuousness make gaudy palettes of his pages:

A feast of moon and men and barking hounds,
An orgy for some genius of the South
With blood-hot eyes and cane-lipped scented mouth,
Surprised in making folk-songs from soul sounds.[13]

*Cane* was experimental, a potpourri of poetry and prose, in which the latter element is significant because of the influence it had on the course of Negro fiction. Mr. Toomer is indebted to Sherwood Anderson and Waldo Frank for much in his prose style, but his material is decidedly his own. Sometimes he falls short of his best abilities for lack of government, as in the story "Kabnis," which says and does much but obscures much more. Sometimes he succeeds splendidly, as in the sketches "Carma" and "Fern," in which feeling and language are restrained and genuine. But often he wallows in feeling and grows inarticulate with a rush of words.

Though *Cane* was in the nature of an experiment (the conclusion to which we are fearful of never knowing, for since 1923 Toomer has published practically nothing) it established the precedent of self-revelation that has charac-

terized the writings of Negroes on all levels ever since. At
first completely absorbed in fulfilling his opportunity for release, the new Negro had no time for new forms. In his anx-
iety and relief he did not reflect that he was pouring new
wine into old bottles. In truth, he was somewhat distrustful
of his new place in the sun. He was afraid of being a fad,
the momentary focus of the curiosity of dilettantes, charla-
tans, and student sociologists. It was common sense for him
to attempt to establish himself on something more solid than
the theatrical reputation of Florence Mills or the *bizarreries*
of what many people thought to be the Greenwich Village
influence. New forms were faddish froth : material the marrow. And what more arresting material than the self-reveal-
ing truth!

Thus by 1924 the new movement was definitive and hard.
Jessie Fauset, whose first novel, *There Is Confusion*, appeared
in 1924, gave the precedent added validity. Perhaps because
she was a woman and a little shocked at the kind and quality
of truth in Toomer, she deserted Toomer's people and his
type of revelation, choosing the cultivated Negro society of
Philadelphia and New York for her milieu. Her race pride
did not turn to the Negro's heritage in the soil, but to his
heritage in ancient lineage and in culture. The result was
that her characters are so commonplace as to seem actual
transcriptions from unimaginative life, and her novels often
bear a striking resemblance to the duller novels of white
middle-class society. The novelist herself states the case in
the foreword to *The Chinaberry Tree:*

"But of course there are breathing-spells, in between spaces
where colored men and women work and love and go their
ways with no thought of the [race] 'problem.' What are they
like then? So few of the other Americans know. . . . His
forebears are to him quite simply the early settlers who
played a pretty large part in making the land grow. He

boasts no Association of the Sons and Daughters of the Revolution, but he knows as a matter of fact and quite inevitably his sons and daughters date their ancestry as far back as any. So quite as naturally as his white compatriots he speaks of his 'old' Boston families, 'old Philadelphians,' 'old Charlestonians'. . . . Briefly he is a dark American who wears his joy and rue very much as does the white American. He may wear it with some difference, but it is the same joy and rue."

It was with this always in mind that Miss Fauset wrote not only her first novel and *The Chinaberry Tree*, but *Plum Bun* and *Comedy: American Style* as well. No other Negro novelist so thoroughly offsets the artificial glamor associated with the Negro by such novels as *Nigger Heaven*, *The Blacker the Berry*, *Prancing Nigger*, and *Sweet Man*. The deeper problem of all Miss Fauset's novels is of course race, and yet her Negro characters are no more concerned with it than are the white characters who occasionally enter. Treatment of this kind gives the problem an incidental air, avoids the heavier going of propaganda, and at the same time makes it serious enough to command attention. Her novels, too, leave no room for doubt that the new Negro meant to go beyond mere self-revelation. From that moment in *There Is Confusion* when Peter Bye enters, bringing with him the complexities of racial dependence and interdependence, we realize that the novelist is trying to say something and get somewhere.

§ 3

From the elemental hysteria of Langston Hughes's "Saturday Night"[14] to the chilled and competent beauty of Helene Johnson's "Fulfillment"[15] is a long flight of song, not always perfectly sustained and not always perfectly suited to the tableaux to which it is instrumental. But the tableaux do not suffer from this. They suffer rather by reason of their own limitations.

The stage is crowded with figures, so crowded that eventually their attitudes and postures come to seem cramped and artificial. It was crowded long before Arna Bontemps reinspired the half-legendary men and women of *Black Thunder*, to add others to an already extraordinary pageant. There are Claude McKay's black roustabouts, Jake and Banjo, who roved the world like giants; there are the degenerates, the parasites, the vampires who slunk through Wallace Thurman's slimy demi-world; there are the courageous but futile professional men and women of Walter White's far South; northern metropolitan centers yield Rudolph Fisher the wholesome, hard-working, fun-loving, cracker-hating laborer, and the religious domestic who works in the white folk's kitchen. Rich man, poor man, zealot, fool, flapper, matron, bigot, prostitute—the ignorant, the intelligent, the wholesome, the foul are there in great numbers and in a variety of attitudes and in a multiplicity of still-born events. A prodigious, revealing pageantry.

One important writer among the new Negroes stands out as having contributed nothing or little to this conglomeration. That writer is the poet Countee Cullen. He for himself (as well as others for him), has written numerous disclaimers of an attitude narrowed by racial influence. He may be right. Certainly *Caroling Dusk*, his anthology of "verse by Negro poets," represents a careful culling of the less distinctive, that is to say, the less Negroid poetry of his most defiantly Negro contemporaries. Nevertheless it remains that when writing on race material Mr. Cullen is at his best. His is an unfortunate attitude, for it has been deliberately acquired and in that sense is artificial, tending to create a kind of effete and bloodless poetry in the manner of Mr. Braithwaite. The essential quality of good poetry is utmost sincerity and earnestness of purpose. A poet untouched by his times, by his conditions, by his environment is only half a poet, for earnestness and sincerity grow in direct proportion as one feels intelligently the pressure of immediate life. One may not like the pressure and the necessities under which it forces one to labor, but one does not deny it. Donne, as he grew older, oppressed by the thought of his ultimate physical decay and the weight of his (often imaginary) sin, wrote of God and repentance. Aseeth with the romantic notions of the French revolution, Wordsworth elevated all of nature, including man, to a common kinship in the Divine. Now undoubtedly the biggest, single unalterable circumstance in the life of Mr. Cullen is his color. Most of the life he has lived has been influenced by it. And when he writes by it, he *writes;* but when this does not guide him, his pen trails faded ink across his pages.

To argue long about Countee Cullen—his ideas, his poetic creed, and the results he obtains—is to come face to face with the poet's own confusion. It is not a matter of words or language merely, as it was with Dunbar: it is a matter of ideas and feelings. Once Mr. Cullen wrote: "Negro verse (as a designation, that is) would be more confusing than accurate. Negro poetry, it seems to me, in the sense that we speak of Russian, French, or Chinese poetry, must emanate from some country other than this in some language other than our own."[16]

At another time: "Somehow or other I find my poetry of itself treating of the Negro, of his joys and his sorrows— mostly of the latter—, and of the heights and depths of emotion which I feel as a Negro."[17]

And at still another:

> Then call me traitor if you must,
> Shout treason and default!
> Saying I betray a sacred trust
> Aching beyond this vault.

I'll bear your censure as your praise,
For never shall the clan
Confine my singing to its ways
Beyond the ways of man.[18]

The answer to all this seems to be: Chinese poetry translated into English remains Chinese poetry—Chinese in feeling, in ideas.

But there is no confusion in Mr. Cullen's first volume, *Color*,
which is far and away his best. Here his poetry (nearly all
of it on racial subjects, or definitely and frankly conditioned
by race) helps to balance the savage poetic outbursts of
Claude McKay. Countee Cullen is decidedly a gentle poet,
a schoolroom poet whose vision of life is interestingly dis-
torted by too much of the vicarious. This lends rather than
detracts. It is as if he saw life through the eyes of a woman
who is at once shrinking and bold, sweet and bitter. His
province is the nuance, the finer shades of feeling, subtility
and finesse of emotion and expression. Often however, with
feline slyness, he bares the pointed talons of a coolly ironic
and deliberate humor which is his way of expressing his resentment at the racial necessities.

Once riding in old Baltimore,
    Heart-filled, head-filled with glee,
I saw a Baltimorean
    Keep looking straight at me.

Now I was eight and very small
    And he was no whit bigger,
And so I smiled, but he poked out
    His tongue, and called me, "Nigger."

I saw the whole of Baltimore
    From May until December;

Of all the things that happened there
That's all that I remember.[19]

Again, in "To My Fairer Brethren" :

Though I score you with my best,
    Treble circumstance
Must confirm the verdict, lest
    It be laid to chance.

Insufficient that I match you
    Every coin you flip ;
Your demand is that I catch you
    Squarely on the hip.

Should I wear my wreathes a bit
    Rakishly and proud,
I have bought my right to it ;
    Let it be allowed.[20]

When he leaves work of this kind for the heavier moods
and materials so popular with Hughes, McKay, Horne,
Alexander, and *The Crisis* and *Opportunity* poets, Mr. Cullen
bogs down. He is the Ariel of Negro poets. He cannot beat
the tom-tom above a faint whisper nor know the primitive
delights of black rain and scarlet sun. After the fashion of
the years 1925-1928, he makes a return to his African heritage, but not as a "son returned in bare time." He was not
among the Negroes who were made Africa conscious and
Africa proud by the striding Colossus, Marcus Garvey, by
Vandercook's *Tom-Tom*, and O'Neill's *The Emperor Jones*.
Cullen's gifts are delicate, better suited to bons mots, epi-
grams, and the delightfully personal love lyrics for which a
large circle admire him.

The title poem of his third volume, *The Black Christ*, illustrates at once the scope and the limit of his abilities. Bitter and ironic in its mood, revealing but slight narrative and dramatic powers, the poem is feeble with the childish mysticism of a bad dream, penetrating the realm of emotional reality no more than does a child's relation of a nightmare. Here in this poem Mr. Cullen's lyricism is smothered, his metrical faults exaggerated, and his fear of stern reality italicized.

§ 4

The fact that the new Negro had something to say was not completely swamped in his mania for self-revelation. Jessie Fauset's novels and the better poems of Countee Cullen give definite voice to an increasing store of ideas, opinions, and conclusions. Walter White's melodramatic novel, *The Fire in the Flint*, and his painstaking study, *Rope and Faggot*, both examinations of certain aspects of the social order, get at the mind by way of the emotions. Robert R. Moton, then principal of Tuskegee, made an attempt to catalogue and explain Negro thought on almost all the important relations of mankind. George Schuyler's incisive mind cut through many a fog bank of wishful, wistful reverie. The short stories and the first novel of Rudolph Fisher, the most talented narrative artist in the group, under all their technical skill and appearance of mere cleverness say things to the mind. Dr. DuBois, silent for a time, except in the pages of *The Crisis*, thought aloud in *Dark Princess*.

What did the new Negro have to say? What was he thinking? Truth to tell, he was becoming a first-class cynic with decidedly red tendencies. First of all, he deserted the church, that staunch bulwark of bourgeois conservatism, in great numbers. He started laughing at religion, and many began to use it merely as the tool of charlatanism. He lost rapidly all sense of ethical progression and, like his white contemporaries, acquired an exaggerated sense of the value of what he called economic stability. The Republican party became no longer the only party, for through deflection to the Democrats the Negro passed on to Socialism, Communism, and even Nihilism. Though he laughed at the gaudy uniforms, jeered the unmanned and rotting ships of the Black Star Line, and derided the Utopian ideas of the leader of the Universal Negro Improvement Association, he was shocked by Marcus Garvey.[21] He was shocked, alarmed, amazed at the gigantic demonstration of the herd instinct, and confused, confounded, and humiliated by the public disclosures of graft and incompetence. His illusions crashed about him. The hounds of inferiority bayed on his trail. He began to believe that but two ways were left open to him : the bitter indifference that begins the end, and escape—escape through conformity (possible only to the white-blacks), or through desertion of the "American way," or through absolute and unequivocal submission, or through atavistic reversion.

Most of this brooding thought was nourished by the work of certain white writers whose books have had a wide public since 1925. Certainly Julia Peterkin's *Black April* and *Scarlet Sister Mary*, with their return to old concepts and stereotypes (which she helped revive), did not further the Negro's self-respect. Dowd's pseudo-scientific *The American Negro* gave an air of authenticity to the utterances of the prejudiced southern press. The savage primitivism of DuBose Heyward's Porgy, Crown, and Bess, and of Eugene O'Neill's Brutus Jones seemed to indicate that the Negro was no more than a brute, while Carl Van Vechten's polite, light *Nigger Heaven* pictured him as absorbing all the vices and none of the virtues of white civilization.

In various guise the futility, the pessimism, the atavism began to appear in the literature of the new Negro. Langston Hughes might declare in extenuation, as he did in 1926, that the new Negro was bent upon writing what he wanted

to write, that he stood, as it were, free on the mountaintop;
but he did not mention that even there on the mountaintop he breathed the noxious air of desperation ascending
from the valley. Not in joy but in desperation did the same
poet write :

> Me an' ma baby's
> Got two mo' ways,
> Two mo' ways to do de Charleston!
>    Da, da
>     Da, da, da!
> Two mo' ways to do de Charleston!
>
> Soft lights on the tables,
> Music gay,
> Brown-skin steppers
> In a cabaret.
>
> White folks, laugh!
> White folks, pray!
>
> Me an' ma baby's
> Got two mo' ways,
> Two mo' ways to do de Charleston![22]

Nor did he try to be brave and laughing with that bitter
desperation of joy when he wrote :

> We cry among the skyscrapers
> As our ancestors
> Cried among the palms in Africa
> Because we are alone,
> It is night,
> And we're afraid.[23]

Hughes is the most prolific and the most representative of the new Negroes. By training and experience he is at the opposite end from Cullen, that is to say, he is a Negro divinely capable of realizing (which is instinctive) and giving expression to (which is cultivated) the dark perturbation of the soul—there is no other word—of the Negro. There is this difference between racial thought and feeling : what the professors, the ministers, the physicians, the social workers think, the domestics, the porters, the dock hands, the factory girls, and the streetwalkers feel—feel in a great tide that pours over into song and shout, prayer and cursing, laughter and tears. More than any other writer of the race, Langston Hughes has been swept with this tide of feeling. This accounts for the fresh green of him, the great variety of his moods. "The tom-tom laughs, the tom-tom sobs," and between laugh and sob there is a scale of infinite distinctions.

But there is artifice, the cultivated, in him too. Certain of his pieces like "Cabaret" and "Saturday Night" quite evidently are tomfooleries as to form, but other pieces showing the strong influence of the midwestern poets are seriously experimental. Unless we consider as experiments the short stories of Frances Ellen Watkins and her retention of dialectal patterns without the dialect speech sounds, Negro writers had never experimented with form, and none since Dunbar had seriously tackled the problem of language. Mr. Hughes, more concerned with form than language, interested himself in a poetic design that would fit his material. The result is the Blues and the Shout. To the first he has given a strict poetic pattern ; "one long line repeated, and a third line to rhyme with the first two. Sometimes the second line in repetition is slightly changed and sometimes, but very seldom, it is omitted." The Shout also has a pattern, definite but flexible. It takes its name from the single line of strophic and incremental significance which is shouted or moaned after each two, three, or four line stanza. There is also evidence that Mr. Hughes more recently has been experimenting with short story forms.

Mr. Hughes's experiments do not touch his more deeply moving verse. Is it that the bizarre forms, like the bizarre language of dialect, impose limitations upon expression? When he wishes to get beyond these, Mr. Hughes resorts to the purer verse forms as in "The Negro Speaks of Rivers," "Cross," and "I, Too." Certainly none of the Blues, no matter how full of misery, and none of the Shouts, no matter how full of religion, ever get beyond a certain scope of feeling. He can catch up the dark messages of Negro feeling and express them in what he calls "racial rhythms," but it is as the iteration of the drum rather than the exposition of the piano. He feels in them, but he does not think. And this is the source of his naïvete.

But Langston Hughes is not all naïvete either. His short stories are a case in point. The title story of his volume of stories, *The Ways of White Folks*, and such stories as "Cora Unashamed" and "Camp Meeting" are caviar to the general. Such stories as these map the broad highways of indifference, of primitivism, of futility down which the Negro artist is escaping to his end—or his beginning. The beautiful black Cora, unadapted and unadaptable, was lost in the complexities of a society of which she should have been a part. Mr. Hughes, if you will, makes us see how undesirable such a society is, but the fact remains that the individual must conform to society. It is victory to live in Rome. Cora knew neither victory nor defeat—simply nullification. And it is the same with the characters in the novel *Not Without Laughter*. Aunt Hagar is as the door between that world from which the Negro had struggled since slavery, the world of poverty, of strife, of the inescapable consequences of being black, and that other world of smug physical comforts, of middle-class respectability into which her daughter Tempy had passed as into heaven. But to the other daughters, Annjee and Harriet, Tempy's world is no more satisfactory than their own. They do not want these imitation worlds of white folks' making.

This same futility becomes blank despair in the novels of Nella Larsen. The chief personages of *Quicksand* and *Passing*, white to all superficial appearances, attempt to find life across the line. Helga Crane of *Quicksand*, she of the Swedish mother and the Negro father, is driven back by hereditary primitivism; first in a Stockholm theater where she hears two American Negroes singing the blues and jazz of Harlem, and then in a Harlem feast of prayer:

"As Helga watched and listened, gradually a curious influence penetrated her: she felt an echo of the weird orgy resound in her own breast: she felt herself possessed by the same madness: she too felt a brutal desire to shout and fling herself about. Frightened by the strength of the obsession, she gathered herself for one last effort to escape, but vainly. In rising, weakness and nausea from last night's unsuccessful attempt to make herself drunk overcame her. She fell forward against the crude railing which enclosed the little platform. For a little moment she remained there in silent stillness, because she was afraid she was going to be sick. And in that moment she was lost,—or saved. The yelling figures about her pressed forward, closing her in on all sides. Maddened, she grasped at the railing and with no previous intention began to yell like one insane, drowning every other clamour while torrents of tears streamed down her face. She was unconscious of the words she uttered, or their meaning: 'Oh, God, mercy, mercy. Have mercy on me!' but she repeated them over and over." And in the end she goes with sadistic ruthlessness to her final, sordid defeat. Clare Kendry, the heroine of *Passing*, who though married into the white race makes periodic returns to her own, seeks escape in death, in a horrible and unpremeditated suicide.

Dr. DuBois's *Dark Princess* has been mentioned already for its delineation of the defeatist attitude. Eric Walrond's *Tropic Death*, Wallace Thurman's *The Blacker the Berry*, Countee Cullen's *One Way to Heaven*, and Walter White's *Fire in The Flint* are no different in kind. Even the prose of Claude McKay, with its sensationalism and its melodramatic devices (which have caused it to be said that he writes with too thoughtful an eye on the white-consumer public), is made morbid by the futilistic speculations of Ray in *Home to Harlem* and *Banjo*, and nauseating by the atavistic reversion of the young teacher-preacher in *Banana Bottom*.

> Each page into the book of life I turn
> I view as ashes of a cankered urn.

Two bright spots relieve the Stygian depths of the picture drawn by most of the new Negro novelists: one is the satire *Black No More*, by George Schuyler, and the other is the comedy-romance *The Walls of Jericho*, by Rudolph Fisher. That Mr. Schuyler could poke fun and Dr. Fisher could laugh amid the dreary wastes of psychopathic imaginings is evidence that all measure of sanity was not gone.

## § 5

What happened in Negro literature from the appearance of Van Vechten's *Nigger Heaven* in 1926 until 1935 is obvious. First of all, Negro writers, both poets and novelists, centered their attentions so exclusively upon life in the great urban centers that the city, especially Harlem, became an obsession with them. Now Harlem life is far from typical of Negro life; indeed, life there is lived on a theatrical plane that is as far from true of Negro life elsewhere as life in the Latin

Quarter is from the truth of life in Picardy. The Negro
writers' mistake lay in the assumption that what they saw
was Negro life, when in reality it was just Harlem life. Very
shortly, for literary purposes anyway, Harlem became a sort
of disease in the American organism.

Again, it was not upon the New Yorker (as distinguished
from the Harlemite) that the Negro writers concentrated.
Driven by the restless demons of their own forebodings,
doubts, despairs, they sought the food necessary to the ap-
petites of these spiritual and intellectual furies. The very
things that caused their illness they fed upon. They needed
whores, pimps, the sweetmen; *bistros*, honky-tonks, spider-
nests; the perverse, the perverted, the psychopathic. They
found them, of course, in abundance. In this it might be
said, somewhat in extenuation, that they seemed to follow
fashion.

It is to this last—the following of fashion—that certain
critics would affix all the blame for what it has pleased one
of them to call "the degraded literature." But it was more
than just fashion: the thing the new Negro followed was
soul-deep. Popular writers follow the fashions in literature
in order to make money. No one of the new Negroes can
be accused of making money, or even of wanting to make
money. Langston Hughes was undoubtedly right when he
declared of the younger Negro artists: "If the white people
are pleased, we are glad. If they are not, it doesn't matter.
. . . If colored people are pleased, we are glad. If they are
not, their displeasure doesn't matter either."[24] It just happened that *Nigger Heaven* created a variation on a demand
that the Negro writers were spiritually and psychologically
prepared to fill. This literature would have been anyway.
Some of it, as a matter of fact, had been written before *Nigger Heaven*. It is literature of escape. Literature of escape becomes necessary to a people in times of great moral and so-

cial stress. McKay and Hughes, Thurman and Larsen were no more immune to the catastrophic pressure of the war and the changes with which its aftermath affected their common lot than were Faulkner and Hemingway, Remarque and Sherriff safe from such pressure and the changes in their own lives. Negro mothers, too, bore children into the "lost generation."

There is something of wonder in the fact that a quiet little book of brilliant poems appearing in 1927 was not overlooked. The book was *God's Trombones: Seven Negro Sermons in Verse*, and its author was James Weldon Johnson. Like its foremost contemporaries (*Fine Clothes to the Jew* had appeared the same year and *Weary Blues* the year before), *God's Trombones*, too, made a return to the primitive heritage, but not in the sensational and superficial way of the younger writers. "The Creation" and "Go Down Death," two of the seven sermons, are among the most moving poems in the language and certainly rank with the best things done by American Negro poets. But it is not enough merely to say this, for it explains nothing of another significance.

In 1917 Mr. Johnson's first volume of poems, *Fifty Years*, was published. A section of this book was called "Croons and Jingles" out of consideration for the limitations of the dialect the author used in such pieces as "Sence You Went Away":

> Seems lak to me de stars don't shine so bright,
> Seems lak to me de sun done loss his light,
> Seems lak to me der's nothin' goin' right,
>     Sence you went away.

Under this section also Mr. Johnson made limited use of folk material. *The Book of American Negro Poetry* was issued in 1922. It was not nearly so definitive as the title implies, but

Mr. Johnson's preface as editor indicates that he had given important thought to folk material and its mode of expression. In that scholarly essay he said: "What the colored poet in the United States needs to do is something like what Synge did for the Irish. . . . He needs a form that is freer and larger than dialect, but which will still hold the racial flavor; a form expressing the imagery, the idioms, the peculiar turns of thought and the distinctive humor and pathos, too, of the Negro, but which will also be capable of voicing the deepest and highest emotions and aspirations and allow of the widest range of subjects and the widest scope of treatment." This same preoccupation is also evident in Mr. Johnson's preface to *The Book of American Negro Spirituals*.

Then came *God's Trombones* as a brilliant example of the maturing of his thoughts on folk material and dialect. Aside from the beauty of the poems, the essay which prefaces them is of the first importance for it definitely hails back from the urban and sophisticated to the earthy exuberance of the Negro's kinship with the earth, the fields, the suns and rains of the South. Discarding the "mutilations of dialect," Mr. Johnson yet retains the speech forms, the idea patterns, and the rich racial flavor.

> O Lord, we come this morning
> Knee-bowed and body-bent
> Before thy throne of grace.
>
> .    .    .    .    .    .    .
>
> And now, O Lord—
> When I've done drunk my last cup of sorrow—
> When I've been called everything but a child of
>     God—
> When I'm done travelling up the rough side of the
>     mountain—

O—Mary's Baby—
When I start down the steep and slippery steps of
    death—
When this old world begins to rock beneath my
    feet—
Lower me to my dusty grave in peace
To wait for that great gittin' up morning.[25]

But more important still is Mr. Johnson's acknowledg-
ment of his debt to the folk material, the primitive sermons,
and the influence of the spirituals, for it is undoubtedly Mr.
Johnson's return to these things that has influenced the
gratifying new work of Sterling Brown in poetry and Zora
Neale Hurston in prose. What Mr. Johnson has said of
Sterling Brown in the preface to *Southern Road* might also be
said (and Miss Fannie Hurst nearly says it) of Zora Hurston's *Jonah's Gourd Vine* and *Mules and Men*. Mr. Johnson
said: "For his raw material he dug down into the deep
mine of Negro folk poetry. He found the unfailing sources
from which sprang the Negro folk epics and ballads such as
'Stagolee,' 'John Henry,' 'Casey Jones,' 'Long Gone John'
and others. . . . He has made more than mere transcriptions of folk poetry, and he has done more than bring to it
mere artistry; he has deepened its meaning and multiplied
its implications."

To understand what Mr. Johnson means, to know how
this new work differs from the old, one has only to read such
things as "Southern Road," "When De Saints Go Marching Home," "Frankie and Johnny," and "Memphis Blues,"
quoted below:

I

Nineveh, Tyre,
Babylon,
Not much lef'

Of either one.
All dese cities
Ashes and rust,
De win' sing sperrichals
Through deir dus' . . .
Was another Memphis
Mongst de olden days,
Done been destroyed
In many ways . . .
Dis here Memphis
It may go;
Floods may drown it;
Tornado blow;
Mississippi wash it
Down to sea—
Like de other Memphis in
History.

II

Watcha gonna do when Memphis on fire,
  Memphis on fire, Mistah Preachin' Man?
Gonna pray to Jesus and nebber tire,
  Gonna pray to Jesus, loud as I can,
    Gonna pray to my Jesus, oh, my Lawd!

Watcha gonna do in de hurricane,
  In de hurricane, Mistah Workin' Man?
Gonna put dem buildings up again,
  Gonna put em up dis time to stan',
    Gonna push a wicked wheelbarrow, oh, my Lawd!

Watcha gonna do when de flood roll fas',
  Flood roll fas', Mistah Gamblin' Man?
Gonna pick up my dice fo' one las' pass—

Gonna fade my way to de lucky lan',
Gonna throw my las' seven—oh, my Lawd!

### III

Memphis go
By Flood or Flame;
Nigger won't worry
All de same—
Memphis go
Memphis come back,
Ain't no skin
Off de nigger's back.
All dese cities
Ashes, rust. . . .
De win' sing sperrichals
Through deir dus'.[26]

Certainly the first and second sections of *Southern Road* and
the tales in *Mules and Men* mean something. They mean a
sweet return

In time, for though the sun is setting on
A song-lit race of slaves, it has not set;
Though late, O soil, it is not too late yet
To catch thy plaintive soul, leaving, soon gone,
Leaving, to catch thy plaintive soul soon gone.[27]

It is this that must happen; a spiritual and physical return
to the earth. For Negroes are yet an earthy people, a people
earth-proud—the very salt of the earth. Their songs and
stories have arisen from a loving bondage to the earth, and
to it now they must return. It is to this, for pride, for strength,
for endurance, that they must go back. Sterling Brown says
it in "Strange Legacies":

Brother,
When, beneath the burning sun
The sweat poured down and breath came thick,
And the loaded hammer swung like a ton
And the heart grew sick ;
You had what we need now, John Henry.
Help us get it.

# NOTES

CHAPTER I. THE FORERUNNERS

1 Oscar Wegelin, *Jupiter Hammon*, Heartman's Historical Series, No. 13, New York, 1915.

2 "An Address to the Negroes of the State of New York," in *ibid.*

3 *Ibid.*

4 "To the Right Honorable William, Earl of Dartmouth, His Majesty's Secretary of State for North America," *Poems.*

5 "On Liberty and Slavery," *Poems by a Slave.*

6 *Poems.*

7 Anonymous, *Memoirs and Poems of Phillis Wheatley, a Native African and Slave: Also, Poems by a Slave.*

8 "Praise of Creation," *Hope of Liberty* and "On Liberty and Slavery," *Poems by a Slave.*

9 "Heavenly Love," *Hope of Liberty.*

10 Untitled. Bound with an undated sheaf of anonymous poems, all apparently written by slaves. Quoted by Vernon Loggins, *The Negro Author*, New York, Columbia University Press, 1931.

11 "On Hearing of the Intention of a Gentleman to Purchase the Poet's Freedom," *Poems by a Slave.*

12 "On the Truth of the Saviour," in *ibid.*

13 "Creditor to his Proud Debtor," *Naked Genius.*

CHAPTER II. LET FREEDOM RING

1 Benjamin Brawley, *A Social History of the Negro*, New York, 1921.

2 *Ibid.*

3 Speech untitled. Quoted by William Wells Brown, *The Black Man*, New York, 1863. *The Black Man* is a hodge-podge of history, biography, and anecdote.

4 *Men of Mark*, Cleveland, 1887.

5 *Narrative of William Wells Brown*, pp. 44-46.

6 "Speech at Rochester, July 5, 1852," Carter G. Woodson, *Negro Orators and Their Orations*, Washington, 1925.

7 A letter in possession of Miss Ann Hamilton of Louisville, Kentucky, lineal descendant of Thomas Hamilton.

8 This is unlisted in any bibliography. It was issued without date, printer's name, and publisher's imprint, apparently privately printed for circulation among the author's audiences. The small, paper-back volume can be found in the Harris Collection of American Poetry in the Brown University library.

9 *Poems*, Philadelphia, 1871.

10 *Ibid.*

11 *Poems*, Philadelphia, 1895.

12 "Song for the First of August," *Poetical Works of James Madison Bell.*

13 Introductory note to "The Progress of Liberty," *Poems.*

14 Introductory note to "The Emancipation of Slaves in the District of Columbia," *Poems.*

15 "The Progress of Liberty," *Poems.*

CHAPTER III. ADJUSTMENT

1 George E. Haynes, *Trend of the Races*, New York, 1922.

2 Constance Rourke, *American Humor*, New York, 1931.

3 Harry T. Burleigh (ed.), *Plantation Melodies Old and New*, New York, 1901.

4 *Complete Poems of Paul Laurence Dunbar.*

5 "Signs," *'Weh Down Souf and Other Poems.*

6 This can be found in the Harris Collection of American Poetry in the Brown University library.

7 "Emancipation," *'Weh Down Souf and Other Poems.*

8 "Skeetin' on de Ice," *'Weh Down Souf and Other Poems.*

9 "The Poet," *Complete Poems of Paul Laurence Dunbar.*

10 Introduction to *Lyrics of Lowly Life.*

11 "A Song," *Complete Poems of Paul Laurence Dunbar.*

12 Preface to *The Book of American Negro Poetry*, ed., James Weldon Johnson.

13 "Two Little Boots," *Complete Poems of Paul Laurence Dunbar.*

14 In *ibid.*

15 "Sonnet on an Old Book with Uncut Leaves," in *ibid.*

16 In *ibid.*

17 Booker T. Washington, *Up From Slavery*, p. 121.

18 "Speech at the Atlanta Exposition," Carter G. Woodson, *Negro Orators and Their Orations.*

19 *Darkwater.*

20 *The Souls of Black Folk.*

21 *Ibid.*

22 *Ibid.*

23 *Ibid.*

24 "Hymn of Hate," *Darkwater.*

25 "A Litany of Atlanta," *Darkwater.*

26 "The Scarlet Woman," *The Book of American Negro Poetry*, ed., James Weldon Johnson.

27 "Tired," in *ibid.*

28 "Children of the Sun," in *ibid.*

29 *Saint Peter Relates an Incident.*

30 James Weldon Johnson, "Fifty Years," *Fifty Years and Other Poems.*

31 Can be found in *Caroling Dusk.* Mr. Braithwaite wrote this sketch in the third person. To avoid confusion, I have taken the liberty to change the pronouns to the first person.

32 Jessie Fauset, "Noblesse Oblige," *Caroling Dusk.*

33 "Sandy Star and Willie Gee," *Sandy Star and Willie Gee.* Can be found in *Caroling Dusk.*

CHAPTER IV. EMERGENCE OF THE
NEW NEGRO

1 George E. Haynes, *Trend of the Races*, New York, 1922.

2 "Lift Every Voice and Sing," *Saint Peter Relates An Incident.*

3 "The New Negro," *Independent*, Jan. 15, 1921.

4 *Harlem Shadows.*

5 Associated Publishers, Washington, D. C.; Dill and DuBois, New York.

6 *American Mercury*, December, 1928.

7 *Songs of Jamaica*, London, 1911.

8 "The Tropics in New York."

9 Angelina Grimke, "Surrender," *Caroling Dusk.*

10 Leslie P. Hill, "My Race," *Wings of Oppression.*

11 Paul Rosenfeld, an essay on Toomer in *Men Seen.*

12 "Song of the Son."

13 "Georgia Dusk."

14 *Weary Blues.*

[15] *Opportunity*, June, 1926.

[16] Preface, *Caroling Dusk*.

[17] *Copper Sun* (inside back cover).

[18] "To Certain Critics," *Color*.

[19] "Incident," in *ibid*.

[20] *Color*.

[21] Marcus Garvey and the Universal Negro Improvement movement fired a large part of the Negro population of the country for a four or five year period (1919-24) and so seriously threatened a kind of race-revolution that a Federal probe was made of Garvey's activities. He was tried and convicted on Federal charges and sentenced to five years at Atlanta. His followers yelled "frame-up" (they were strong politically) and finally he was released and deported to British West Indies (Jamaica) from whence he had come. Nearly every week the Negro press has news of Garvey. He still heads the movement and he seems still to have plenty of energy.

[22] "Negro Dancers," *Weary Blues*.

[23] "Afraid," *Fine Clothes to the Jew*.

[24] "The Negro Artist and the Racial Mountain," *Nation*, June 16, 1926.

[25] "Listen, Lord," *God's Trombones*.

[26] Sterling Brown's *Southern Road*.

[27] Jean Toomer, "Song of the Son," *Cane*.

# BIBLIOGRAPHY

Arnett, Benjamin William. "James Madison Bell." Preface, *Poetical Works of James Madison Bell*. San Francisco, 1901.

Baker, Ray Stannard. *Following the Color Line*. New York, Doubleday, Page, 1908.

Bell, James Madison. *Poetical Works*. San Francisco, 1901.

———. *Poems*. Lansing, 1903.

Bontemps, Arna. *Black Thunder*. New York, Macmillan, 1936.

Braithwaite, William Stanley. "Sandy Star and Willie Gee," *Caroling Dusk*. New York, Harper, 1927.

———. *The Poetic Year for 1916; a Critical Anthology*. Boston, Small, Maynard, 1917.

Brawley, Benjamin. *A Social History of the Negro*. New York, Macmillan, 1921.

Brown, Sterling. *Southern Road*. New York, Harcourt, Brace, 1932.

Brown, William Wells. *Clotel; or, The President's Daughter*. London, 1853.

———. *Clotelle; a Tale of the Southern States*. Boston, 1864.

———. "Miralda ; or, The Beautiful Quadroon. A Romance of American Slavery. Founded on Fact." New York, *Anglo-African*, 1860-1861.

———. *My Southern Home; or, The South and Its People*. Boston, 1880.

———. *Narrative of William W. Brown*. Boston, 1847.

———. *St. Domingo: Its Revolutions and Its Patriots*. Boston, 1855.

———. *The Black Man, his Antecedents, his Genius, and his Achievements*. Boston, 1865.

———. *The Escape; or, A Leap for Freedom*. Drama in Five Acts. Boston, 1858.

———. *The Negro in the American Revolution. His Heroism and His Fidelity*. Boston, 1867.

———. *The Rising Son; or, The Antecedents and Advancement of the Colored Race*. Boston, 1874.

———. *Three Years in Europe: or, Places I Have Seen and People I Have Met*. London, 1852.

Burleigh, Harry T. *Plantation Melodies Old and New*. New York, Schirmer, 1901.

Carmichael, Waverly. *From the Heart of a Folk*. Boston, Cornhill, 1918.

Chesnutt, Charles Waddell. "Baxter's Procustes," *The Atlantic Monthly*, June, 1904.

———. *The Colonel's Dream*. New York, Doubleday, Page, 1905.

———. *The Conjure Woman*. Boston, Houghton Mifflin, 1899.

———. *The House Behind the Cedars*. Boston, Houghton Mifflin, 1900.

———. *The Marrow of Tradition*. Boston, 1901.

———. *The Wife of His Youth and Other Stories of the Color Line*. Boston, Houghton Mifflin, 1899.

"Common Sense," Anonymous. Date unknown. (Circa, 1897.)

Cullen, Countee. *Caroling Dusk*. An anthology. New York, Harper, 1927.

———. *Color*. New York, Harper, 1925.

———. *Copper Sun*. New York, Harper, 1927.

———. *One Way To Heaven*. New York, Harper, 1932.

———. *The Black Christ*. New York, Harper, 1929.

Davis, Daniel Webster. *'Weh Down Souf and Other Poems*. Cleveland, 1897.

Douglass, Frederick. *Life and Times Of Frederick Douglass*. Hartford, 1881.

———. *My Bondage and My Freedom*. New York, 1855.

———. *Narrative of the Life of Frederick Douglass, an American Slave*. Boston, 1845.

———. *The Constitution of the United States: Is it Pro-Slavery or Anti-Slavery?* (Pamphlet.) Halifax. Undated.

Dowd, Jerome. *The Negro in American Life*. New York, Century, 1926.

DuBois, William Burghardt. *Dark Princess*. New York, Harcourt, Brace, 1928.

———. *Darkwater*. New York, Harcourt, Brace, 1920.

———. *John Brown*. Philadelphia, Jacobs, 1909.

———. *The Philadelphia Negro*. Philadelphia, University of Pennsylvania Press, 1899.

———. *The Quest of the Silver Fleece*. Chicago, McClurg, 1911.

———. *The Souls of Black Folk*. Chicago, McClurg, 1903.

Dunbar, Paul Laurence. *Complete Poems*. New York, Dodd, Mead, 1913.

———. *Lyrics of Lowly Life*. New York, Dodd, Mead, 1896.

———. *Majors and Minors*. Toledo, 1895.

———. *Oak and Ivy*. Dayton, 1893.

———. "One Man's Fortunes," *The Strength of Gideon, and Other Stories*. New York, 1900.

———. "At Shaft 11," *Folks From Dixie*. New York, 1898.

———. "Silas Jackson," *The Strength of Gideon, and Other Stories*. New York, 1900.

———. "The Case of 'Ca'line,'" *The Strength of Gideon, and Other Stories*. New York, 1900.

———. *The Fanatics*. New York, Dodd, Mead, 1901.

———. "The Ingrate," *The Strength of Gideon, and Other Stories*. New York, 1900.

———. *The Love of Landry*. New York, Dodd, Mead, 1900.

———. *The Sport of the Gods*. New York, Dodd, Mead, 1902.

———. *The Uncalled*. New York, 1898.

Fauset, Jessie Redmon. *Comedy: American Style*. New York, Stokes, 1933.

———. *Plum Bun*. New York, Stokes, 1929.

———. *The Chinaberry Tree*. New York, Stokes, 1931.

———. *There Is Confusion*. New York, Boni and Liveright, 1924.

Firbank, Ronald. *Prancing Nigger*. New York, Brentano's, 1924.

Fisher, Rudolph. *The Walls of Jericho*. New York, Knopf, 1928.

Grimke, Angelina. "Surrender," *Caroling Dusk*. New York, Harper, 1927.

Hammon, Jupiter. *An Address to Miss Phillis Wheatly* [sic], *Ethiopian Poetess, in Boston, Who Came from Africa at Eight Years of Age, and Soon Became Acquainted with the Gospel of Jesus Christ*. Hartford, 1778.

———. *An Address to the Negroes in the State of New York*. New York, 1787.

———. "A Dialogue, Entitled, The Kind Master and Dutiful Servant," *An Evening's Improvement*. Hartford. Undated.

———. *An Evening's Improvement. Shewing, the Necessity of Beholding the Lamb of God. To Which is Added, a Dialogue, Entitled, The Kind Master and Dutiful Servant*. Hartford. Undated.

———. *An Evening Thought: Salvation by Christ with Penetential Cries:*

*Composed by Jupiter Hammon, a Negro Belonging to Mr. Lloyd, of Queen's Village, on Long Island.* New York, 1760.

———. "A Poem for Children with Thoughts on Death," *A Winter Piece.* Hartford. Undated.

———. *A Winter Piece: Being a Serious Exhortation, with a Call to the Unconverted: and a Short Contemplation on the Death of Jesus Christ.* Hartford. Undated.

Harper, Frances Ellen. *See* Watkins, Frances Ellen.

Harte, Rollin. "The New Negro," *Independent*, January 15, 1921.

Haynes, George Edmund. *Trend of the Races.* New York, Federal Council of Churches, 1922.

Heyward, DuBose. *Porgy.* New York, George H. Doran Co., 1925.

Hill, Leslie Pinckney. *The Wings of Oppression.* Boston, Stratford, 1921.

Horton, George Moses. *Hope of Liberty.* Raleigh, 1829.

———. *Naked Genius.* Raleigh, 1865.

———. *Poems By a Slave.* Philadelphia, 1837.

Hughes, Langston. *Fine Clothes to the Jew.* New York, Knopf, 1927.

———. *Not Without Laughter.* New York, Knopf, 1930.

———. *The Ways of White Folks.* New York, Knopf, 1934.

———. *The Weary Blues.* New York, Knopf, 1926.

Hurston, Zora Neale. *Jonah's Gourd Vine.* Philadelphia, Lippincott, 1934.

———. *Mules and Men.* Philadelphia, Lippincott, 1935.

Johnson, Fenton. *A Little Dreaming.* Chicago, Peterson, 1912.

———. *Songs of the Soil.* New York, The Author, 1916.

———. *Visions of the Dusk.* New York, The Author, 1915.

Johnson, Helene. "Fulfillment," *Opportunity*, June, 1926.

Johnson, James Weldon. *Black Manhattan.* New York, Knopf, 1930.

———. *Fifty Years and Other Poems.* Boston, Cornhill, 1917.

———. *God's Trombones : Seven Negro Sermons in Verse.* New York, Viking, 1927.

———. "Introduction," *Southern Road*, by Sterling Brown. New York, Harcourt, Brace, 1932.

———. "My City," *Caroling Dusk.* New York, Harper, 1927.

———. *Saint Peter Relates an Incident*, New York, Viking, 1935.

———. *The Autobiography of an Ex-Colored Man.* Boston, Sherman, French and Co., 1912. New ed., New York, Knopf, 1927.

———— (ed.). *The Book of American Negro Poetry*. New York, Harcourt, Brace, 1922.

———— (ed.). *The Book of American Negro Spirituals* (With J. Rosamond Johnson). New York, Viking, 1925.

————. "The Dilemma of the Negro Author," *The American Mercury*, December, 1928.

Johnson, Julia H. *The Negro Problem*. New York, 1921.

Johnson, J. Rosamond. *The Book of American Negro Spirituals* (With James Weldon Johnson). New York, Viking, 1925.

Jones, Joshua Henry. *The Heart of the World*. Boston, Stratford, 1919.

Larsen, Nella. *Passing*. New York, Knopf, 1929.

————. *Quicksand*. New York, Knopf, 1928.

Lee, George Washington. *Beale Street*. New York, Vail-Ballou Press, 1934.

McKay, Claude. *Banana Bottom*. New York, Harper, 1933.

————. *Banjo*. New York, Harper, 1929.

————. *Harlem Shadows*. New York, Harcourt, Brace, 1922.

————. *Home to Harlem*. New York, Harper, 1928.

————. *Songs of Jamaica*. Kingston, Jamaica, 1912.

————. *Spring in New Hampshire*. London, 1920.

*Memoir and Poems of Phillis Wheatley, a Native African and Slave: Also, Poems by a Slave*, Anonymous. Boston, Light, 1838.

Millen, Gilmore. *Sweet Man*. New York, Viking, 1930.

O'Neill, Eugene. *The Emperor Jones*. New York, Appleton, 1921.

Peterkin, Julia. *Black April*. Indianapolis, Bobbs, Merrill, 1927.

————. *Scarlet Sister Mary*. Indianapolis, Bobbs, Merrill, 1928.

Rosenfeld, Paul. *Men Seen*. New York, Dial Press, 1925.

Rourke, Constance. *American Humor*. New York, Harcourt, Brace, 1931.

Schuyler, George. *Black No More*. New York, Macauley, 1931.

Seligman, Herbert J. *The Negro Faces America*. New York, Harper, 1920.

Simmons, William J. *Men of Mark: Eminent, Progressive and Rising*. Cleveland, 1887.

Thurman, Wallace. *The Blacker the Berry*. New York, Macauley, 1929.

Toomer, Jean. *Cane*. New York, Boni and Liveright, 1923.

Vandercook, John W. *Tom-Tom*. New York, Harper, 1926.

Van Vechten, Carl. *Nigger Heaven*. New York, Knopf, 1926.

Walrond, Eric. *Tropic Death*. New York, Boni and Liveright, 1926.

Walker, David. *Walker's Appeal, in Four Articles; together with a Preamble to the Colored Citizens of the World, but in Particular and Very Expressly to those of the United States of America*. Boston, 1829.

Washington, Booker T. *Up From Slavery*. New York, Doubleday, Page, 1901.

Watkins, Frances Ellen. *Iola Leroy; or, Shadows Uplifted*. Philadelphia, 1893.

———. *Moses: A Story of the Nile*. Philadelphia, 1869.

———. *Poems*. Philadelphia, 1871.

———. *Poems*. Philadelphia, 1895.

———. *Poems on Miscellaneous Subjects*. Philadelphia, 1893.

———. *Sketches of Southern Life*. Philadelphia, 1873.

———. *The Sparrows Fall and Other Poems*. Without plates. Undated.

Wegelin, Oscar. *Jupiter Hammon*. New York, Heartman's Historical Series, No. 13, 1915.

Wheatley, Phillis. *Poems*. Boston, 1827.

———. See *Memoir and Poems of Phillis Wheatley*.

White, Walter. *Rope and Faggot*. New York, Knopf, 1929.

———. *The Fire in the Flint*. New York, Knopf, 1924.

Woodson, Carter G. (ed.). *Negro Orators and Their Orations*. Washington, Associated Publishers, 1925.

# INDEX